HOLY BALLYHOO

Effective Publicity
For Your Church

Oren Arnold

HOLY BALLYHOO

ISBN 0-89536-100-0
PRINTED IN U.S.A.

Whenever three beautiful and talented young matrons dedicate their lives to Christ in happy, spirited manner, not only are their families blest, but the whole nation takes a step forward. Wherefore, this book is dedicated with love to my daughters
   JUDY O'REILLY
      ROSIE DETWILER
         GAIL TUREK

ACKNOWLEDGEMENT

Literally hundreds of dedicated, talented persons helped with enthusiasm in the development of this book. The author is grateful to all of them. His very special thanks go to the Rev. Dr. Norman Vincent Peale, the Rev. Dr. Albert O. Hjerpe, the Rev. Dr. Robert H.Schuller, the Rev. Dr. George H. Hall, the Rev. Dr. Billy Graham, the Rev. Dr. Arthur J. Tankersley, the Rev. Dr. Charles R. Ehrhardt, the Rev. Dr. Morgan Odell who is a retired President of Lewis and Clark College, the late Rev. Dr. Charles S. Poling, the Rev. Mr. Aaron Powers, the Rev. Mr. Roy Shepler, the Rev. Mr. Eldon H. Thies, the Rev. Mr. Arthur Chartier; also to George W. Crane, M.D., Ph.D., to Mr. Ralph D. Yates and his wife Raffaella, who typify the very young generation of lay church workers, as do Mrs. Judith O'Reilly and her husband Patrick, Mrs. Rosemary Detwiler and her husband Jerry, Mrs. Ruby Schmieder and her husband Otto, Mrs. Delores "Bunny" Neece who is a skilled and very modern church secretary and her husband Robert who is an avid church worker; also to Robert and Jeanne Decker, young retirees whose seven years in England brought valuable insight about publicity techniques there; and surely to my own beloved teammate Adele R. Arnold, who is virtually a cornerstone of our own big and modern-minded church.

— O.A.

CONTENTS

THE BASIC PREMISE

Virtually all branches of industry or "business" (such as General Motors, Westinghouse, IBM, whiskey distillers, cigarette manufacturers, gasoline companies, local groceries, and department stores, even small shops) allocate a minimum of **five percent of their anticipated gross revenue** each year for advertising and/or "public relations." Five percent, to sell their products to the people.

The Christian church has the greatest of all "products" to sell — salvation, with its happy way of life.

But the Christian church (a composite of many small "retail" outlets) allocates less than one tenth of one percent of its anticipated revenue, its annual budget, to advertising and public relations.

Shame on us!

For our inefficiency; our neglect of opportunity; our failure to use the honest and effective selling techniques of our time.

Jesus himself used the techniques of his era, as a man among men.

Why are we so negligent?

How can we today help our clergy "sell" the glories of Christianity to the multitudes?

Read on . . .

THE APPROACH ...
Your Preliminary Thinking

The very thought of "advertising" our religion is shocking to millions of us. It would be blasphemy; wholly out of keeping with the solemnity, piety, and dignity associated with worship since history began. The Good News is too sacred to be defiled with wild displays in newspapers, or with garish billboards and super-silly television commercials. **Christianity should be spread by word of mouth in direct person-to-person testimony.**

Agreed!

SHOULD be.

COULD be. In fact, has been; but only to a tragically limited extent.

Most of us feel personally inept at it. We sense our lack of training in how to approach people individually even though we are told that God will put the right words in our mouths. If we force it, strain at it, we tend to become fanatical, making nuisances of ourselves by ringing too many doorbells and talking tactlessly. Thus most of us turn shy or lose confidence in our skill at personal evangelism. So we cast about in our yearning, seeking better ways.

We soon come to realize that professional expertise is called for in helping Christianity to spread.

The ideal, of course, is to have a Norman Vincent Peale or a Billy Graham personality for pastor. Quite a few churches across America and Canada, perhaps fifty or more of them, do have pastors who, by sheer force of enthusiasm and dedication, draw in multitudes. Yet all those experts have their detractors; many lesser pastors as well as many laymen tend to criticize and belittle them.

It is my opinion, based on prolonged national study, that this belittling stems primarily from envy, or plain old narrow-mindedness. One lay critic, hearing a great evangelist, said to him after a highly successful worship service, "I do not like your methods of teaching Christianity." Gently, lovingly, but devastatingly, the evangelist squelched him by replying, "I do not think they are very good myself. **What are yours?**"

What are yours, indeed! What are mine? It is a haunting question that each of us individuals must face. For every organized church group it is even more powerful and inescapable.

Other distinguished names come to mind. Almost surely you can remember a few yourself, right now, because along with Peale and Graham they have become nationally renowned.

Foremost among the modern standout pastors may be the Rev. Dr. Robert H. Schuller, at Garden Grove, California. This man is something of a modern-day prophet; and in whimsy, you can even make that "profit" if you wish. Truly he is phenomenal.

He was so innovative, so imaginative and driven with enthusiasm, that he developed a tiny flock of forty into a membership now nearing 10,000 — one of the largest anywhere, ever. His first sermon to the forty was spoken from the roof of an abandoned theater. Today the multitude assembles at a huge, almost overwhelming tabernacle. It does not "look like" a church at all. There are beautiful buildings, grouped around not a conventional steeple, but a high tower in which are offices. A trickling stream runs through the courtyard. There is a vast outdoor space where people may sit right in their cars and worship, hearing the sermon via small radios that are provided, much like a drive-in movie. His pulpit, stationed dramatically high above his indoor audience, has an electric button that he can touch.

After the morning processional, he does touch that button, whereupon a high, magnificent screen of water fountains along one great glass wall slowly recedes. The glass doors there silently slide open, and the people out there in their cars in effect become united with those many worshipers in their pews. Wonderful! **"I am the church, you are the church, we are the church together!"**

All of that is consummate showmanship-publicity, unmatched anywhere. It constantly gets talked about; **of course** it does!

You think maybe all of that is too **too**? Somewhat overly flambuoyant? You don't like Schuller's methods of publicizing the word of Christ? Okay, brother or sister, I repeat — what are yours?

But we aren't done with Schuller yet. At the time of this writing, his church is already "The Vatican of The Protestants." Schuller didn't say that, George W. Crane did, in 1976. Crane has an M. D. and a Ph. D. and is undoubtedly America's foremost psychiatrist-psychologist. Crane's daily column (on successful Christian living as individuals and as families) is syndicated to more hundreds of newspapers than is the work of any other writer, not even excepting "Dear Abby" Van Buren who is herself a fine God-loving woman. For years Dr. Crane taught the world's largest Sunday School class in Chicago. He still lectures widely across the nation, is in fact probably the world's foremost "publicity expert" for the Christian way of life. So if a man of **his** stature calls Bob Schuller's church "The Vatican Of The Protestants," you can believe it!

Moreover, as this is written, even that existing Protestant "Vatican" is being replaced. In its place, Schuller's great flock is erecting what may become the largest, most impressive, most beautiful, and probably most influential, house of worship in human history.

It will be an all-glass structure reaching far and soaring very high, in restrained modernistic styling. It will show nothing but windows to the outside world, at least 10,000 of them — imagine! The projected cost? At least $500,000,000; half a billion dollars. It has already been named — The Crystal Cathedral.

Its potential impact on humanity is staggering. It is "publicity" at its best. It tells the world that Christians are not mealy-mouthed do-nothings, cringing in the boat of life. True, not all churches everywhere can ever hope for such grandeur, and they don't need to. But in proportion, every church group everywhere, even those in the "Wild Wood" or the backwoods, can catch the gleam for efficient upgrading in its own area. Every flock, large or small, has its gifted men and women, boys and girls. They can develop a local Reach Out program which is not handicapped by puritanical restraint and tradition just as Peale, Graham, and Schuller are doing on a big scale.

New, evangelistic type ministers seem to arise every few months. Some become flashes in the pan and little else; they soon return to obscurity. Others — usually less prone to collect a fortune in money — discover that they have a powerful influence, especially on what are called the Common People, which means the good-hearted Johns and Marys who are slugging it out in the economic battle trying to earn a decent living for their families. So called sophisticates do not often respond to evangelism.

One eager fellow who stayed with it is Oral Roberts. He found that he had a gift of speech, a personality which pleased most people. So, **he** has become nationally renowned. Now he even has a university named for him, with a powerful sports program as well as high-level scholarship. Nice! And do not "yes but" me about him, or about any similar leaders; I do not wholly like his methods, either, and yet — what are mine?

Those four Big-Name pastors (and others comparable) are backed by tremendously successful publiciy build-up campaigns, ongoing day to day, month to month, year by year. Hundreds of millions of dollars, plus countless man and woman hours, are spent on their various forms of "advertising."

Those four are so famous that they can barely change a shirt without a headline or a newscast resulting. (But then, a poor woman, incurably ill, just touched the cloak of another Great Minister and **was** cured, therby creating a "news release" still being re-read and re-broadcast 2,000 years later.

Now we must, perforce, add a fifth standout Personality.

This one is a layman. For years he was virtually a nobody, a country hick type; nice enough but — well, you know — kind of seedy and RFD. All right, so time streamed on. Then suddenly that strange combination of circumstances, which strikes unpredictably in many lives, elevated him.

Well, I'm not a Southern Baptist, though my pappy was and we raised some peanuts of our own, in a village smaller than Plains. Also I am a revoltin' Republican — if that's any business or interest of yours. But my attention surely was captured.

The first shock wave was one of pride; I like to see a good old country boy in overalls honored by the people. Then suddenly, I felt indignation; our boy had admitted (in a despicable pornographic magazine) that yes, he had lusted, had sinned. Horrors!

But the fact was — is — that there have been only three perfect Americans: you . . . and me . . . and offhand I forget just who the third one is. So I decided not to "judge" him. And was gratified when he himself said that he had prayed for forgiveness, and gotten it because he **believed**. I went right into my darkened den and whispered some prayers of my own.

That country boy also taught Sunday School and admitted it nationally — imagine! On television, he told the world of sophisticates that **love** is important, and he did it with solemnity, with no cynicism; didn't even flash the famous smile. Washington was astounded. His proclamation triggered a sort of political, sociological, ecumenical groundswell across the nation, and use of the word "love" became fashionable again. Millions of us of every age began to dust off our Bibles.

Publicity?

For Christianity? For "the church?" For love and morality and decent all-American living in general?

WHOO-WEEEEEEEE, you better believe it!

Never mind about his fundamentalism or whatever. Never mind about tradition and dignity and pietistic pomposity and all that old guff. This was not formalistic prayer-wheel turning. Just look at what sincerety and audacious "public relations" did for the man. There's no comparable instance in all our history.

All of this does not imply that we have to approve of everybody else's techniques used in promoting Christianity. We are quite right to take a dim view of evangelism that is too agressive, too prone to "judge," too rigid and categorical in its beliefs. I live on the Pacific shore, and am often appalled at what many of us call "the kooks of California." Our sunkist state attracts thousands of weirdos and susceptible persons, the unthinking ones, the immature minded. These are tragically exploited by opportunists offering strange, concocted "religions," new ones every few months, mostly for monetary gain. Also I am completely fed up with members of that sect who persistently ring my doorbell and tell me I am doomed if I do not worship precisely as they do. And I think of another sect, non-Christian, whose little bands of promotors shave their heads, wear saffron-colored robes, ring tiny bells, chant repetitiously and incessantly as they parade our downtown sidewalks. Often they harass shoppers and merchants to such an extent that legal action must be taken to halt them; whereupon they proclaim themselves to be martyrs.

That sort of zeal, of course, is pure fanaticism. It is not at all what Jesus meant when he said go forth and spread the Word. He assumed that we would use at least some measure of common sense. He gave us the know-how; taught us the psychology of tenderness — which modern psychologists declare is the one indispensable emotion; taught us love and gentleness and quiet dignity; taught us to **identify** with people, not dictate to them or harangue them.

Oh yes indeed, personal zeal is imperative, is absolutely the Number 1 way to spread Christianity. As with selling a car or a horse, a dress or a house, that ultimate person-to-person contact is the clincher. This can (and usually does) begin with the clergyman, then is passed on through parents to children and friend to stranger, thus streaming down the centuries.

But in selling today, the preliminary buildup can help immeasureably in making the prospective buyer receptive, "softening" him for the sale.

This buildup is called publicity, or public relations, or advertising, or — a catch phrase — holy ballyhoo. The methods are almost endless in number and variety and effective avenues of use. Properly applied, they bring good results that are absolutely astounding.

The truly great need, of course, is for **all** the churches of all the respected and honored faiths to unite in a national public relations campaign, to "sell" our North American nations (and ultimately the world) on the basic tenets of morality and godliness;

not on a basis of fear, but as a matter of simple intelligence, and of exhilarating life enjoyment. All of us — proclaiming goodness and decency, and showing exactly why this is imperative. Moreover, such a project is not too much to hope for, pray for, plan for; certainly among Christians and Jews, who have a common need, and are infinitely strong, this idealistic dream can become reality soon! Let every individual give it a push.

But meanwhile — each "retail" outlet (church or synagogue) can start an effective campaign of its own, in its individual sphere of influence. Many of the holy ballyhoo techniques are available even to the smallest, poorest congregation.

In describing them here my temptation at first was to go all-out serious, which so many people feel is the only correct-and-reverent way to discuss a religious subject. But second thoughts — plus some careful manuscript testings — impelled me to forget about that doctoral-thesis style, worshiped by the academicians. Such a formal or pedantic technique would have killed the effectiveness of the book. I want it to be read and **enjoyed** by a more typical stratum of society. I want it to make sense not only to the Archbishop of Canterbury, but equally to the pastor deep in the backwoods heart of Texas. After all, I was not born in Blenheim Palace; I was born and reared in a log house in a tiny East Texas village (Minden) 12 rutty miles from any railroad, and may God forever bless the memory of the people who surrounded me there.

— O. A.

Chapter 1

YOUR LOCAL NEWSPAPER

This is Tuesday morning.

The good Reverend Mr. or Dr. Prototype and his staff have planned what they hope will be a truly grand gathering in the sanctuary Sunday after next. All the Sunday School classes will be there. The music will be exceptionally good, the order of worship will be very special. That would be a perfect day to have non-members, sinners from all levels, attend and see Christians in mass worship, with a follow-up invitation to join them. Please, dear God.

But how to get the visitors in?

Somewhat wistfully, wishfully, Dr. Prototype thinks first of the town's leading newspaper. He knows it to be a Force. It **must** be, because announcement of a football game fills the high school stadium. And is football as important as a gathering to worship God? Yes, the paper **must** be a Force, because the merchants spend many thousands of dollars advertising their wares in it and they wouldn't keep that up year after year if the public didn't respond. Well, then?

Almost pitifully he calls in his secretary. "Uh, Mary Lu, could you — would you please write up a little something for **The Daily Clarion,** and drop it off there on your way to lunch? About our forthcoming big mass meeting?"

"Of course, sir."

Mary Lu is a doll of a person. A sweetheart. A Christian. Loved by everybody. Full name? Mrs. Mary Louise Willinghorse. Her late husband, Henry Willinghorse, was killed in an accident that left her virtually destitute. Her qualifications for being a pastor's secretary and the public relations expert for her church? She was willing; and she needed the money to live on and support her little girl. Bless Mary Lu.

I am not sneering, not being flippant.

I, too, love Mary Lu. As a Session member, I even voted to pay her a fabulous $500 a month, pledging some of it myself. I knew her as a child. She never finished high school, but did take a four-month training in business college, learning typing, shorthand, and what was called Basic Grammar. Her mother was my wife's friend.

Wherefore, on this Tuesday morning Mary Lu laid aside everything else for a few minutes and prepared what she called a write-up for the paper. Here it is, word for word:

> There will be a special meeting in the Downtown Church of The Chimes. ALL PLEASE COME. The Sunday School classes will all be there and a special collection will be taken for the poor. Dr. Prototype's sermon topic will be "O Prepare Ye." It is hoped that many strangers will attend. The organ has been repaired and Mrs. Norris has recovered and will sing. She has been down with bronkitys. Come one, come all.

Now don't you dare laugh at that.

Because it is not funny, it is tragic.

In fact, it is the exact wording of a "write up" taken to a real newspaper in a real town by a real secretary from a real church. Worse yet, it is all too typical of hundreds, thousands, hundreds of thousands, of "write ups" dutifully and hopefully sent to newspapers every week across the Christian world. Ask any editor.

"The Paper" Ranks First

When any of us seeks publicity for almost anything, we think first of the local newspaper. We have been conditioned toward that for at least 100 years. We have inherited the belief that if something is **printed** it is believable and motivating, it is an important truth. That was the secret of the old-time medicine man, who printed cures for everything from dandruff to cancer on his bottles, although they contained nothing but water, alcohol, and vegetable coloring.

Another plus factor for the paper is that a news story is **on record.** We can refer to it again and again. Thousands of church secretaries are required to clip every item published about their churches and paste them in albums "for future reference." Somehow or other we hold that to be important, although if truth be known, it isn't. Careful samplings and studies show that such records are almost never actually referred to, never really needed. They are, in fact, second in unimportance only to "the minutes of the last meeting" so faithfully kept and all but worshiped by the church social clubs and similar groups, and which are promptly filed and forgotten. If, by chance, it ever does become important to refer to a newspaper article published last month or last year or last decade, about a church matter, then it is far easier and cheaper to have sweet Mary Lu drop by **The Clarion** office and look it up in the paper's own indexed files, a ten-minute effort.

But the people in most church offices do not reason in such manner. Whatever is printed in "the paper" is **ipso facto** important, or it wouldn't have been printed in the first place. That very belief, however, is mistaken, shallow thinking, because a great portion of any newspaper's content is mere trivia. Even so, habit patterns are strong. So then — the paper. For the big church meeting, a write-up in The Paper.

This attitude holds whether it is a four-page weekly in Hillsboro, Indiana, pop. 800, or a 100-page issue of **The Times** in New York City, pop. 8,000,000. George W. Crane, M.D., Ph. D., lives in the small village, Hillsboro. Quite incidentally, he is a nationally renowned Christian psychologist, whose writings are syndicated to some 400 newspapers, and who for years taught the world's largest Sunday School class (in nearby Chicago). I am proud to call him my personal friend. And I know that he is delighted if any sermon or Christian guidance he delivers is "written up" in the regional paper. Similarly, our fellow Christian in New York City — Norman Vincent Peale — is delighted if the great **New York Times** "writes up" something he says or that his Marble Collegiate Church does. In fact, he maintains a vast public-relations organization (at nearby Pawling, N.Y.) promoting Christianity as he sees and proclaims it. More power to him!

Yes, we stand in awe of The Paper; at least we have done so, up to the 1970's. And truly it is essential for the pastor to understand its modern limitations in prestige and influence. Nevertheless, he must work with his local paper as best he can. Where possible, he must walk a mile in the editor's moccasins. Most good editors do have sympathetic hearts for what the pastor and his church are trying to do; because they too had mothers, they too probably were exposed to Sunday School as kids. Most newspaper reporters and editors work exceedingly hard. They are underpaid. They are harassed; pressured from without, nagged from within by their own consciences and wisdom. They need Christian friendship and guidance, and secretly yearn for it despite any surface cynicism that shows.

Why, therefore, did Mary Lu's little "write up" not appear at all in the local **Clarion**? Much to her and Dr. Prototype's disappointment.

The answer is quite clear: Mary Lu's manuscript was amateurish, even childish.

It lacked even the simple basics of a news story; it gave no date for the special church meeting, it gave no address for the church itself although a plea was made for strangers to attend; it used trite phrases (Come one, come all); it barely hinted at the meeting's importance, no promise of reward for attending; it even had a comically misspelled word.

Quite naturally, almost any editor anywhere would have smiled his thanks at Mary Lu — who is quite pretty — would have glanced at her little paper, and later filed it in his wastebasket. Or, at best, would have revised it and printed it as a one-inch filler near the bottom of page 4. Kindly Dr. Prototype, of course, had day-dreamed of seeing something impressive printed under a big headline on Page 1.

Bless all the beloved Dr. Prototypes of this world, who have only gentle Mary Lus to turn to when publicity is needed. The same thing would have happened if a comparable "write up" had been sent to the prestigious **Los Angeles Times** — one of the world's great newspapers, circulation about 1,000,000, readership averaging four times that.

No paper can really afford to send a skilled reporter around to the church to gather facts and do a professional job of writing about a Sunday meeting, no matter how important that meeting may be in the pastor's mind.

A Reporter For The Church

It's a problem for Dr. Prototype.

It is also a problem for the ruling elders, session, deacons, priests, rectors, vicars, bishops, rabbis, whatever the control group may be called.

They meet often in solemn conferences about the matter of getting free publicity in the papers, a problem that has existed for many years.

There is a solution:

Hire a trained newspaper writer to prepare the news stories.

HIRE him (or her); don't ask for free service. You get what you pay for in this life — remember?

Never mind what you think he **ought** to do, without pay. Who are you to judge that? In a sense, the preachers themselves ought to work without pay; the secretaries, organists, and sextons ought to work without pay. But people have to eat; and their decisions about **giving** are strictly personal ones, not for you or the church staff or the ruling body to force on any person. "I always thought religion was free," says a fine old legend, about a man who protested when the collection was taken. "Yes," replied the pastor, "religion **is** free. But you have to pay for the piping." Just like rainwater, piped into your home! A deep psychology enters here. If you **ask** that professional writer for free service, you might get one-time or short-time service of high quality. But if you pay him even a modest amount, **he becomes your boy,** his conscience becomes a driving force, he feels obligated, knowing he will be rewarded honorably for work honorably done, as an ongoing project. Precisely as you, Reverend Sir, feel obligated to give your best-possible ministry, when paid.

So — hire a smart high school senior student of journalism; better yet, a college journalist. If your congregation holds a professional reporter from the local paper, arrange a moonlighting fee for that one, to handle all church news. If you have no reporter member, go to the paper editor and ask him to recommend some talented staff member who might like to earn something on the side while still serving the paper. In short — search out your talented man or woman for this job.

The payment need not be excessive; just fair. But it will truly impel the writer to do a professional job — or if it doesn't, then fire him! Business is business. Find a good one.

The good one will do all the basics which the editor demands. In addition, he will inject imagination and enthusiasm into every project — no, not fictionizing imagination, but appreciative imagination, seeing the forthcoming big church rally (or whatever) as a rewarding experience for the readership, pointing up the ways in which a stranger can benefit by attending and taking part. Enthusiasm is always contagious. It can grip even the hard-boiled editor; after which he will print the announcement, probably under a two-column headline or larger. It will then grip the readers, and a percentage of them will inevitably respond. They have been offered something not merely "good" in the religious sense, but good in the personal sense, something enticing, promising; something packaged well in print, hence likely to be packaged well in presentation. Which — come to think on it — throws the matter right back in the laps of the pastor and his staff: **make that big rally meeting high class in every way, be sure that it more than lives up to the publicity brag!** This is extremely important. Anything else is dishonest, disillusioning, and disappointing.

No, do not berate Mary Lu.

She was hired to be a secretary, she made no claim to being a public relations expert.

She is a **good** secretary, who takes a load off Dr. Prototype. Both she and he must realize that press agentry is a highly specialized skill, one of the most highly specialized in our world today. It makes or breaks any industry. It even makes or breaks any President. It is an imperative in virtually every endeavor of our lives, because it can indeed figuratively move mountains. Thus, it is stupid not to have it done for our beloved church, by the most skilled hands we can hire. So hire your press agent and pay him well.

"But where will the money come from?" somebody always asks, when I lecture in this vein, as I often do.

I have already answered that in the Basic Premise, at the front of this book. The money will be there when you allocate a minimum of five percent of your annual church budget to publicity. And if you spend that wisely, it will be returned to you tenfold.

Back Up and Begin Anew

In point of cold fact, that "special meeting" so dear to Dr. Prototype's heart would not likely have been publicized in The Paper, no matter who wrote it.

Why not?

Because it had too little to recommend it. The meeting itself became rather dull church routine, unimaginative, non-stimulating. It was simply "doing what has been done," it adhered to tradition, to precedent. But dearly beloveds, this is an Era of Change! Change so incredibly accelerated, that we are suffering now from that future shock about which author Alvin Toffler warned us. What was good for Paul and Silas is **not** good enough for me or you, today. Whether you traditionalists like that thought or not, you have to cope with it. The church does not — ever! — have to change the basic tenets of

Christianity, the ageless Truths of our faith. But it most assuredly does now have to update its methods of disseminating those truths. Millions of our churches are still horse-and-buggy. They didn't even join the horseless-carriage era, and here we are in the shocking jet-space era already yet! We all tend to worship a status quo, whereas it is evaporating right out from under us, every day, because the **rate** of change in our over-all way of life is astronomical.

Does that tell you something, pastor? And ruling laymen of every church?

Today, dear friends, the great Ford Motor Company could not possibly sell a rattly Model T automobile, except possibly as a museum piece. It is selling a sleek new eye-appealing powerful Model Whatever it is called, and even **that** changes every few months!

Is your church program a Model T?

Dr. Prototype's special meeting was ''good,'' but it was old-hat. Those who did attend came more from a sense of ought-to than of want-to. Even if Mary Lu's sweet little write-up **had** been printed, it would not likely have captivated any reader.

If Necessary, Fire Your Pastor

The problem began with that grand gentleman of the Old School — Dr. Prototype himself.

A fine man, he. James John Prototype, fondly called Jimmijohn as a lad growing up in a typical Main Street town. His folks scrimped to put him through college, then three more years in seminary. Handsome now; tall, stately, curly hair that is graying, firm chin, resonant voice, gentle manner, kind hearted, loving and loved, and deeply steeped in the Bible. A saint on earth.

But his sermon topic for the big gathering had been "O Prepare Ye."

Not "bad," it had an overtone of doom. Which dated him at about 1910, when our world was just emerging from Victorian mores and manners.

"O Prepare Ye" holds an ominous warning; perhaps a valid one. Prepare ye, all ye people, for death! Otherwise — hellfire and damnation, instead of wings and a golden harp. Scare tactics!

It completely lacked implementation. It sounded irrelevant to modern folk; something out of grandmother's era. It did not promise us guidance on **how** to prepare ourselves, and assuredly it held out no hint of Good News whatsoever.

It was like father saying to son, "Be good or I will clout you." You can never scare a child into being good, he simply gets sullen and rebellious, then runs away from home — and who can blame the lad? You have to love him and show him how and why he should be good, pointing up the unbelievably grand rewards for it! A **positive** approach — right, Dr. Peale? And Dr. Prototype? Don't frighten me: guide me. Truly, too many preachers still cling to self-imposed authoritarianism. They know the **text** of The Bible, but not the magnificent spirit of it, its inspired guidance toward The Way.

If the preacher in your church is like that, fire him.

If you who read this happen to **be** the preacher like that, fire yourself.

Get out of the profession; or get "with it" for our modern era, as the young people say. The last quarter of this century will not tolerate preaching, teaching, and publicity techniques that were the patterns of the first quarter, or even of the third! This is NOW, pastor! This is a wholly new, swiftly moving, unconventional thinking Point In Time.

Let us assume, therefore, that Dr. Prototype had indeed been hep; that he was a Now person of the Space Age.

His sermon topic for that special big day in church probably would have been something like —

Direct Help in Solving Your Problems

or

Let Us Help You Enrich Your Life

or

All You Have To Do Is Ask

Don't grimace! Don't frown, don't sneer that such sermon topics sound too wild or "modern," implying that they are non-Christian. Don't shrug them off as being "too much like Norman Vincent Peale or Bob Schuller or Billy Graham," whose methods are unconventional. **What are yours?**

Face the grand fact that those titles (or any comparable ones) hold out promise and hope. To a world all too destitute of such grandeurs. There is no "threat," no dire warning; the hellfire-and-damnation assurance for sinners can be sandwiched in later, but it is not good for the theater marquee.

Face the fact that there is divine precedent for such titles. Jesus, the greatest preacher-teacher ever, did not sanctimoniously or dolorously intone "Be good or you are doomed." He did say, for typical instance, "Peace be with you; my peace I give unto you, not as the world giveth give I unto you. Let not your heart be troubled, neither let it be afraid."

Which is to say — in the idiom of the current decade — "I (Jesus) can help you solve your problems, I can help you enrich your life. All you have to do is ask."

Sample Manuscript For Newspaper

Therefore let us now inspect one news manuscript that **might** have been sent to the local editor from Dr. Prototype's Downtown Church Of the Chimes. I have adapted it, with only the names changed from a genuine instance.

Remember, this sample manuscript was not "dashed off" by one of the sweet girls in the church office who had no training in news writing. It was not done by some all-too-common pushy matron volunteer, who secretly aspired to be an author. (Avoid her, by all means!) It was not dictated by the pastor, although it was checked by him and his staff for detailed accuracy.

It was typewritten, double-spaced, with two carbons, on white paper size eight and a half by eleven inches, with two inches left blank at the top, and one-inch margins on the other three sides. Date of requested publication was typed thus in the extreme upper right corner of Page 1: "For release on Thursday June 9." The extreme upper left corner carried this information: "Prepared by (Name of Writer) for the Downtown Church of the Chimes, telephone (number);" that's so the editor could call back for further details if needed. All of the manuscript was meticulously neat; no strikeovers, no misspelled words, no smudgy erasures. In short — it was **inviting** to the editor. One glance told him that it had been written with skill and held some importance.

Here was the text (which you are welcome to adapt for application anywhere):

Direct help in solving your personal or family problems will be offered to the entire community, without charge, at a very special gathering of the people next Sunday, June 12, at 10 a.m. in the Downtown Church of The Chimes, on the 400 block of Maple Avenue. The Reverend Dr. James John Prototype, his choirs, soloists, and counseling staff, have spent more than a month in preparation for this unique event.

Non-members, strangers in our town, tourists, newcomers of every age and status, will be especially welcomed, the church has announced.

"Every man, woman, and child is beset with one or more serious difficulties," said Dr. Prototype, who is widely known for his effective counseling and personality outreach. "Our Christian program, based on divine teaching — not mere preachments or stuffy exhortations — can help anybody face up to any personal problems and triumph over them.

"Despairing persons, of any age and type, are especially welcome; those people who feel themselves at wit's end, or without hope. We guarantee a warm and friendly gathering, a memorable experience, with lasting help. Come as families, or as individuals. There is no charge."

Dr. Prototype's talk from the pulpit, he emphasizes, will not be a conventional sermon. It will be a teaching experience, scaled for simplicity and ease of understanding. It is titled "All You Have To Do Is Ask." That becomes a direct, personal invitation, says he.

Too many millions of folk, he adds, do not bother to "ask." He points out that in our modern materialistic, pseudo-sophisticated patterns of living, we neglect the inner being until we feel embarrassed, or helpless, or even angry.

"When our bodies get sick," this gentle clergyman explains, "we willingly go to a doctor of medicine and put our full trust in him. It is much more important to ask for help where there is a spiritual sickness. And the 'cures' can be much more important, in fact, they can be astounding. There are some incurable physical ills, yet we can help you outface even those; there are no incurable spiritual ills."

Dr. Prototype is among the most highly honored clergymen in his denomination, especially for his direct personal ministry, his kindly guidance for troubled persons. He has been very active in local community life, working with unhappy or unfortunate people at every level.

The June 12 program at his church will be broad screen. It will include special events by and for children, teen-agers, singles, marrieds, parents. Dr. Prototype will endeavor to help any person see a new light, a new exhilarating hope, discovering exactly what should be done about any difficulty. He and his associates then will offer any necessary follow-through assistance, as required.

As usual in this church, the meeting in the sanctuary at 10 a.m. will be followed by a Friendly Time on the beautiful patio there. Coffee and tea will be served to adults, punch to children. Dr. Prototype and his two assistants will be mingling with the people, getting personally acquainted. Special private counseling can be arranged, on request.

Detailed information may be obtained by telephoning the church office, 830-6761.

Impact!

Note that the above news "story" (papers call all their factual reports "stories") is relatively short. It runs less than two typewritten pages, double-spaced. Many news stories run two to six times that, some even more.

But that one has impact!

It is long enough to merit a two-column headline. And in fact, a real one almost exactly like it was published with photos, all under an eight-column, page 2 "banner" headline that read —

What's YOUR Problem? Church Of The Chimes May Have Solution

Now, pause and think.

Who could resist that headline? (All headlines are written by the editors, not by the authors.)

In fact, guess who showed up at that special meeting in the church? The city editor himself! Smiling a bit self-consciously, he admitted that he hadn't attended church in more than a year. Tactfully, the pastor invited him to lunch on Monday. Next day they played golf. By the 15th hole the editor had poured out **his** personal problem, and his new friend was able to help him solve it in barely two weeks. Friendship, rapport, brotherly love, sharing, all came naturally into operation. Which is what Christianity is all about — isn't it?

As per routine in that church, everybody who attended that special day was asked to register on a special blank pad found in the pews; name, address, members, or visitor. In this church with membership of 631 persons, 88 "strangers" were registered! That many, responding to the newspaper publicity; that many, quietly hoping for help with their problems.

There is no record of how many actually found that help. But 31 of those 88 joined that church within the next few weeks! That real-life pastor was delighted. Who can say how much more "good" resulted from that one high-level meeting, publicized by that one professionally written news story?

The author of the story was an experienced reporter. He had an excellent "nose for news," meaning that he sensed the direct human interest, the appeal and universality of importance in what the pastor and his associates were trying faithfully to do. The writer made the most of it. And the city editor quickly recognized that here was a church-news story without any trite, shopworn air of sanctimony or dullness. **This** church meeting seemed to promise something sensible and fine for every person in town, especially every sinner! The Sunday program itself more than lived up to the promise; every detail was high level in quality.

The reporter there was a talented young fellow, newly married and struggling, who had been hired for off-time public relations work at the church, for fifty dollars a month. He was worth at least five hundred dollars.

The Follow-Up

You will realize, of course, that all of those 31 new members did not join the church solely because of one article in the paper and one experience in the sanctuary. A very carefully planned follow-up was set in motion.

Within ten days of the Sunday gathering, each of the 88 "strangers" had been quietly contacted both by telephone and in person. Those who called did not ask the prospects to join the church.

No good salesman crowds his prospects, ever; he is courteous, patient, but alert. Only when he senses that the moment is right, does he move in for the kill. Among automobile salesmen, for typical instance, the best possible technique is restraint, quietly **allowing the prospect to sell himself** on the costly new model.

That powerful truth also is the key in selling church memberships.

Many of those 31 had reacted a bit wistfully. Some latent force had been stirred within them, perhaps some memory, some old yearning for goodness dating back to childhood. The psychiatrists tell us that an impulse toward altruism (unselfish concern for the welfare of others; which is what Jesus taught us) is born in every baby on earth. It is what separates man from the animals; the divine spark. In millions of us, sad to say, it never is allowed to develop. In other millions, it does develop, and these fill the churches. Most people do not know the deep psychiatry-psychology involved, but all do have at least latent instincts about the matter. In these, the altruistic impulse often stirs. This happens even to the outlaw in his prison cell, and to the pseudo-sophisticated housewife or husband in the mainstream of affluent society. Thus every human being is a "prospect" for the salesman of salvation.

The prospect for the new car may go back to the dealer three or four times before making up his mind. So, too, may the church-member prospect "look at the merchandise" repeatedly before buying. Meaning, he/she may attend two, five, or a dozen later worship services and other church activities, taking time to be sure. The skilled pastor knows about this trait in human nature, and moves quietly. The blatant evangelist is prone to coerce an instant decision, but his attrition record is tragic. Unless — as in the case of the great Billy Graham — there has been a powerful, costly, ongoing publicity buildup. Yes, some people do experience instant conversion, and do go on to magnificent heights as Christians; many such miracles are on record. But look behind their scenes, and almost invariably they will have been "brainwashed" unconsciously, prepared for the grand Moment by an unwitting pressure of propaganda, **proper** propaganda! Call it publicity, public relations, advertising, holy ballyhoo, whatever you will. Its power is astronomical.

The skilled pastor knows about such traits in human nature better than we laymen can know, because he is trained to recognize and exploit them for good. Thus in his follow-up of prospects he will not overtalk, will not oversell. Any pressurized sell is likely to result in a cooling off and backsliding later. Deep conviction must come before life dedication, and both mature slowly.

In any event, the patient, loving, tactful follow-up, is the finest "public relations" of all. It is the person-to-person method in operation.

In that instance concerning good Dr. Prototype and his Downtown Church Of The Chimes, the setting was a typical American town of about 9,000 population. Note that the pastor was sadly disappointed. But in the real instance, the setting was the same; small-town America. And the results were gratifying indeed, mainly because a man was paid a meager fifty dollars a month to trigger a magnificent effort. **Only** fifty dollars a month had been allocated for church public relations. Yet the annual budget of that church was in excess of one hundred and eighty thousand dollars. Five percent of that amount would be nine thousand dollars. If that amount had been allocated, instead of the meager six hundred dollars per year for publicity — just imagine what might have resulted!

Chapter 2

ARE NEWSPAPERS REALLY IMPORTANT?

Once-upon-a-time in our storybook long ago, newspapers were sacrosanct. Their editors held strong opinions, and expressed them in language frequently so bold as to cause shootouts. Because there was little else to read, "everybody" studied the papers, discussed them in living rooms, on front porches, in saloons, around campfires. Generally, editors were held to be intellectuals, able to set the moral tone of any community.

That tone usually was high. Its hallmark was Truth. A few quick quotes from 100 years ago:

"Edgar Tucker stole a horse and should be hanged. If the jury doesn't say so, then it should be hanged." (No mealy-mouthed circumlocution there!)

"Abraham Lincoln himself said that whenever a people become dissatisfied with its existing government, it has the right to overthrow that government and set up one of its own that is to its liking. That is exactly what the Thirteen Colonies did in 1776, and what we Confederate States tried to do in 1860. But we were condemned and scorned for seeking the same brand of Freedom!" (No need to say in what area that trenchant editorial originated!)

"Colonel Tom Delaney is an unmitigated liar, and our sympathy goes to his poor wife and children. He should be tarred and feathered and run out of town." (Maybe he

should have been at that. We can also think
of some modern liars who —)

"The citizens named below were in the
local church last Sunday, and God bless them.
If those who were missing fail to show up in
church next Sunday, we shall print their
names." (Oh boy!)

That was the heyday of American journalism.
Forthright speech, a sort of two-gun honor, that
commanded at least respect, if not complete
approval, leadership from the press, in an era when
little other entertainment was available. Naturally.
the newspapers back there were important. Their
prestige lasted until about 1900.

But here in the enlightened last quarter of the
sophisticated 20th century, many editors and
publishers are suspect. Never mind why — that's a
long psychological and sociological study in itself. For
our purpose, we simply have to recognize that "The
Paper" of our modern era is more likely to be
tolerated than venerated.

So, what is our cue, what do we professing
Christians do about that, in our effort to publicize and
"sell" a Christian way of life to the masses?

We haven't much choice. We can only reason that
the vast majority of readers now recognize the
materialistic — not idealistic — attitudes of
newspapers in general, and try to work with them as
best we can. No, we will not be two-faced when
doing that. The paper people well know how we feel
about them. They go to great length trying to justify
their materialism, which often becomes plain old
greed. They rationalize that costs today are so
outrageously high they would go out of business if
they **didn't** have the monetary support from tobacco
and whiskey and other destructive products. They are

much like the federal government itself — which prints bold warnings about dangers to health inherent in nicotine, even while subsidizing the growing of tobacco. But we who condemn are also the very ones who permit; for we ourselves are the government.

We church folk have to recognize — rationalize? — that modern papers also print many wonderful things; many brilliant news stories, commentaries, editorials, articles designed to uplift humanity. They do keep us informed about grave dangers, they do expose perfidy in politics (as witness Watergate), they do furnish much grand guidance for living. So, let us say, "Very well, if we can get some publicity about our Christian aims into print, we will at least be joining the **good** side of the newspapers' policies."

We ourselves, all of us citizens everywhere, are much to blame for the newspapers' faults. The editors have simply reacted logically, giving us what we seemed to want, playing up the nerve-shocking news that we ourselves create. This includes not only money-grubbing, but blatant sex and crime and dishonest politics and all the unloveliness of our existence. Small wonder the paper people have acquired a shell of indifference, bordering on contempt. Wherefore, let us not "judge" them; let us, instead, join them when they try to do good. If we rigidly, sanctimoniously stayed out of the newspapers with our church news, we would simply be isolating sinners. Apropos of which, I now quote you that immortal quatrain by Edwin Markham:

> He drew a circle that kept me out —
> Heretic, rebel, a thing to flout.
> But Love and I had the wit to win:
> We drew a circle that took him in.

The Paper's Church Editor

Continuing our dissection of newspapers in order to understand them, let us keep this in mind: In their mellower moments, both publisher and editor pay at least surface tribute to the Church. I think maybe it is more than surface; it probably is that inborn reach for goodness, that altruistic impulse which has been squelched, but that does periodically re-assert itself. A few newspaper people are nominal atheists, but many others do attend church, even if somewhat furtively. I know the main editorial writer of one great daily. He slips in a bit late every Sunday, says nothing, slips out promptly at the end and hurries away without ever "mingling" and fraternizing. He is almost comical with it, and doesn't realize that he gets talked about because of his attitude. He has a brilliant mind, yet seems slightly ashamed or fearful lest some of the supercilious self-deluding bunch at his office will tag him as a genuine Christian.

But for our main interest here — many newspapers, especially the larger dailies, maintain what is called a Church Editor.

Well, bless him! Even if he doesn't really amount to much. Oh yes, he is almost invariably among the paper's topflight intellectuals, so called. He probably went through college and earned at least a Bachelor of Arts degree, possibly a Masters. He may have specialized not merely in journalism but in Literature as well. He still reads good books. He is soft spoken. He often makes speeches for the quieter cultural groups around town. Sometimes he even fills a pulpit as a guest. On the other hand, he does not draw a very good salary. The paper never sends him out on a sudden sensational news break as it does the police reporter. He is a man of inherent dignity, poise, and yes, humility. My guess is that his adrenalin glands are sluggish, too, because he never seems charged up or very energetic or forceful. Generally, he is content to occupy a desk isolated away over yonder in a far corner of the paper's City News Room.

It is he who gets the little "write ups" that the Mary Lus and the Reverend Dr. Prototypes send in.

All too often he has minuscule space in the paper for his church news. A full page on Saturday? More likely, a page at least half filled with ineffective, amateurish display advertisements from the city's many places of worship — a sort of directory: little 2-inch, 4-inch, maybe 10-inch "ads" with zero reader interest. These start at lower right corner of the page and build upward, leaving the editor perhaps a third of the page at upper left, when he really could use four or five full pages.

So, the poor man is forced to cut every church news story to the bone; tiny 14-point headlines over two-inch texts. No room for big headlines. Some weeks, with advertising slacked off, he can crowd in an essay-type thing, a really brilliant piece of writing by himself or something syndicated out of New York. But even that does not "lift" the church page much. Lacking the sensationalism of Page 1, the slanted controversial matter of the editorial pages, the froth of the comic sections, the excitement of the sports section, his page generally is just glanced at and quickly turned.

That sad indictment is not wholly accurate. I was speaking there of the **typical** reader, the harried housewife and nerve-strained husband, the big children bent on amusement. Actually, studies show that the clergymen and many devout church members do indeed read the paper's Church Page. But those folk are **already** active in church, and we need somehow to corral the outsiders. Those church readers are an estimated fewer than ten percent of the paper's total readership. Included among them are the new travelers who, being in town this week and being devoutly religious at home, look at the church page to locate a place of worship which they can attend this Sunday.

This too sketchy picture of the church editor and his situation is given here so that clergymen and new public relations persons may at least partially understand his problems. Only then can they work with him and not feel frustrated, resentful, or angry.

So What's To Be Done?

The smaller papers, especially in the smaller towns, do not often have a Church Editor, as distinguished from the Managing Editor and City Editor. There, as already indicated, the publicity writer must make his approach direct to these latter gentlemen. How effectively he can do that depends much on his and their personalities.

He must not wheedle or whine or beg. He must not go in with tail tucked between legs pleading; must not "moralize" about the matter. He must not breeze in and **demand;** or threaten any form of coercion. ("We will tell our members not to advertise in your paper or even subscribe to it, if you don't print our church news" — a not uncommon but very stupid gambit.)

In short, the church PR (public relations) man or woman must be a diplomat, which simply means have an instinct for ordinary courtesy and friendly understanding. This is the type of "front" man so cherished in industry and sales business everywhere; yours must be capable of much more remunerative employment, hence be motivated partly from a sense of duty and love. Your church membership does not have such a person? Probably not.

But — find one!

An outsider. Discuss the problems with him/her, the **modus operandi** required. As I have suggested earlier, hire one from the paper itself. Or get that talented, ambitious, energetic, consecrated student of journalism from the nearby college. (America seems over-run with colleges nowadays; as with filling stations, there's one on every corner.) In any event — find him. Make it clear that you want ten times as much talent as your church can afford to pay, but that you will try to pay him at least half what he is worth. In short, make it a pleasant transaction, give him a satisfactory amount, for a **carefully specified** routine of service.

That PR person's first move should be to go right into the office of the church editor, or the city editor if there is no church editor, and invite him to lunch. Let the money for this come out of the allocated fund; your operative does need an expense account on top of his salary. If the pastor is in a happy, relaxed, outgoing mood, take him along; but let him pay for his own meal, he already has a good salary. If the pastor is perpetually dour and rigid and authoritarian, leave the lout in his office, for at the newspaper he will do more harm than good, and will contribute nothing helpful at the luncheon table.

Let the PR person be quite open and above board, frankly stating that he, for the church, wants to talk out a better basis of getting acceptable news into print. Let him **ask**, not try to tell, not try to demand or argue or dictate. Let him caution himself to listen more than he talks. In which case he will learn much, not only about the general need of papers in handling church news, but about this particular editor and his personality. Only with that knowledge can the PR person operate efficiently.

His discoveries, his decisions, should be entered in a very private notebook, for his own future guidance.

There can be no standardized, detailed form for this, or I would print it here. That's because each situation is different, and each personality is. But almost always the church editor or city editor will at least **try** to be sympathetic and cooperative — that's his business, his job. He may maintain a surface attitude of make-me-like-it, a sort of defiance or challenge. Very well, then, **make** him like it. By an open, friendly, alert, tactful, sincere approach. He will always respond to that.

"We Are The Church Together"

We are indeed, even though that's a rather sleazy song, as exalted church music goes. (It belongs maybe at church camp for the teenagers, but not in the magnificent sanctuary, where the people should have the very best programming in all areas.) Happily, though, that title sentence is valid; it means that each individual or congregation can cooperate advantageously with others, indeed that each of us has an obligation to do so.

Your fine church simply cannot "go its own way" and refuse to recognize the importance of the competition in town, the other fine places of worship, even those of other faiths. If you try that, your little flock will be like the tiny crab (note that word well!) that comes out into the sun, but quickly retreats into the sand whenever any other creature heaves into sight. You will have a scared, introverted flock, unworthy of any publicity at all.

Do ask your PR expert to **call on** (not merely telephone or write) the pastors, priests, and rabbis at other temples around town, to meet with you some evening; perhaps in a school room or lodge hall or similar so as to be neutral. If you can afford it, feed them; or at least serve what is euphemistically called "refreshments," which for men had better not be pink-tea glop such as females favor. Do some thinking on that.

The PR expert must not **over**sell in this invitation. Yet he should stress the importance and pleasant aspect of such a meeting. When calling with his invitation, he should explain that the topic of discussion is to be HOW WE CAN WORK TOGETHER TO GET BETTER PUBLICITY IN THE NEWSPAPERS, and ultimately develop holy ballyhoo on a broad scale.

The very thought will intrigue most of those clergymen. It may shock a few, but do urge even those to attend and present any negative reactions they may have.

Invite that Important Force — the city editor. And/or the church editor, if any; of all the town's papers. And surely that big boss at the newspaper office, the managing editor. All three of them on any paper will not come, in some cases none will. But almost surely each **will send somebody** to represent his paper — which is what you want. It may be a reporter, perhaps a "mere" cub. Great! That beginner is likely to be suffused with energy and ideas and enthusiasm. So, urge him to take part in the discussions. You as PR person and chairing this imposing gathering, ask him questions. Make notes on what he says.

A good additional hunch here — take Mary Lu along that night.

The Mary Lu secretary at your church, who is adept at shorthand and maybe has access to a good tape recorder. Ask her to "Keep the minutes" of the meeting in detail so that — for once — somebody can read them later and benefit from them. Ask Mary Lu to take part, herself, in the discussions. After all, she is a woman, with sound intuitions and insights, even though she couldn't write a news story.

As PR director, you may be astounded at the results of such a get-together. That's **if.** If you handle it with a firm hand, cutting off superficial chitchat, gently squelching the inevitable gent who tries to preach or pontificate. Get the meeting right down to basics and hold it there, avoiding all wanderings and irrelevancies. Church committee meetings are notoriously the dullest to be found anywhere; so don't you dare let yours get out of hand.

Keep in mind that most church memberships, especially the larger ones, invariably hold many of the town's advertisers, merchants whose money keeps the papers solvent and prosperous. The editors well know that and will react accordingly. But a more important spiritual point is — men (or women) of good will getting together for a high-level Common Cause are **ipso facto** powerful. They can move mountains and divide seas because as the Master himself told us, "Where two or more are come together in my name, there am I." Well then, you can confidently expect superb results.

"Good" Towns and "Bad" Towns

In some towns (and cities) the churches seem to get much more publicity than they do in other places. One wonders why. Investigation reveals nothing very tangible; it's just that "the spirit of God" appears to be much stronger in the successful areas. Towns and cities can be like families — there are "good" ones and "bad" ones, successful ones and failures. Our best guess about that seems to be that the good ones have somehow attracted or developed high-level leadership, take-charge men and women of force and sound judgment. Many factors seem to attract them to those places — climate, business opportunity, environmental beauty, schools, and **churches.** In such municipalities you can just **feel** the aura of superiority when you drive into the suburbs; you know instinctively that here is a fine place to live. In such a place, the churches invariably are active and are dominant in the social stream.

Many other places seem to have accepted a static condition of low order. Yes, their churches are in business, but are merely **there.** If anybody wants to attend, okay. But if on Sunday morning you would rather play golf or go fishing or sit on country club terrace or stay home and mow the lawn or tick the dog or wash your hair or just loaf in the hammock, nothing will be said or done about it, no notice will be taken, no latent conscience will be stirred. An all too common, sad situation.

Obviously, then, in the lively, intelligent towns, the Christian public relations person can expect easy going. In the pitiful ones, he faces a sterner challenge, a glowering bull with sharp horns. But if he is afraid of a bull, he should stay out of the pasture and let a stout-hearted matador take over.

With a powerful and prayerful approach, the mass human conscience, and consciousness, anywhere can be and frequently is stirred by an ongoing "publicity campaign." This is best maintained by a city-wide cooperative effort — one main reason for calling that meeting of all the town's clergymen.

A local genius is needed to spark that. He/she can be found; there are more geniuses in our communities than anyone suspects, even in those "bad towns.' They seldom apply for jobs because they do not recognize their own potentials. But if Dr. Prototype and his ruling board will seek them out with prayer and persistence, miracles can result.

A test run of publicity can be launched by any one church, small or large. Then it can maintain its own publicity while still cooperating with other churches in a city-wide effort which will change "bad" to "good." This can start with the newspapers. But that start is, of course, a mere beginning. In this swiftly-moving modern era there are **many** PR techniques that have nothing to do with "The Paper" at all. These will be explored in subsequent chapters.

Paid Display Advertisements

As I have already indicated, many persons are shocked at the very thought of advertising a church in any manner. Such folk hold that the church is much too sacred to be "sullied" by advertising or any other form of publicity.

But it is precisely this mistaken policy of isolationism, of trying to keep separate from the routine of individual, family and business life, that has handicapped the churches all these centuries. So, before moving into our consideration of paid display, let me point out something:

Jesus himself indulged in national advertising!

He sent seventy disciples ahead of him, two by two, all over the country to publicize his forthcoming sermons in the various towns. Then in endless ways he showed a flair for the dramatic, comparable to that of Hollywood and New York and Washington, and Montreal and London in our day. How about driving out those temple money changers with a whip, for instance? And those loaves and fishes? And that walking on water? Indeed, that telling the stormy seas to be still and being obeyed? His was news spread by word of mouth, the best publicity ever.

Also, consider Elijah. He, too, had a dramatic flair such as modern advertisers use. He boldly challenged wicked Queen Jezebel's 450 prophets of her idol, Baal, whereupon King Ahab advertised the event nationally. Jezebel wanted Elijah dead or alive, but he outwitted her, dared her own priests under her very palace windows to a life-and-death religious experiment! (1 Kings 18). Can you possibly think that wasn't talked about?

Advertising? What is God's lightning but advertising? And his rainbow? And his flowers that attract the bees, that make the honey, that feed the people? **Advertising is simply calling attention to, then motivating.**

Wherefore, dearly beloveds, keep your minds open, and read on —

Before me as I write this is a Saturday morning issue of **The Register,** a very fine newspaper published in the rather All-American city of Santa Ana, California. I chose it because neither the city nor the paper is "too large." Santa Ana is not Los Angeles, New York, or Chicago. But it is like many dozens of other middle-sized cities in America, Canada, England, Australia, and elsewhere, "big" without having the disadvantages of colossalitude — which is a new word on our scene. Santa Ana, and its daily paper, could be called representative of the English-speaking world today.

Page 6 Section 2 of this Saturday paper has an 8-column headline at the top. It is in bold capital letters more than an inch high, done from a reversed engraving so as to make the words white against a black background. At the headline's extreme right is a large open book and a heavenly spotlight shining on it, obviously a Bible. The headline reads IN CHURCH THIS SUNDAY.

Gratifying, isn't it? A homey heart touch. One senses that Santa Ana is a city of good people, successful families. Such news is implicit in that big headline. It also tells us that the editors are a respected part of that happy town population.

And what is below the big bold headline?

The page is solid with paid display. Fifty-four local churches have their advertisements there. Fifty-four!

The page tends to offset the harsh crime news of this Saturday morning, news that sullies Pages one, two, and three of Section One. But that's not all. Those paid "ads" are on a left-half page; across the fold, at the top of page seven, is another bold headline. This one says —

WEEK-END HAPPENINGS IN CHURCHES OF
ORANGE COUNTY

Under that are twenty-four smaller headlines, one and two columns wide; also several "briefs" or short separate paragraphs, about what church folk in the Santa Ana area will be doing or thinking. Some of the headlines read:

CONGREGATIONS UNITE AT WILSHIRE CHURCH
HEBREW UNION COLLEGE CELEBRATION
REAL FAITH SEMINAR SET
MAGAZINE FEATURED AT ADVENTIST CHURCH
RESTORATION OF CHASTITY, MODESTY,
SOUGHT BY CHURCH
PUPPETS PERFORM FOR SUNDAY SCHOOL CHILDREN
POTLUCK DINNER IN LAGUNA HILLS CHURCH
TEMPLE ISAIAH TO DEDICATE TORAH SCROLL
ASSEMBLY SLATES RENEWAL SERIES

There were others, good news from many congregations. And at the bottom were six more paid display advertisements by churches.

We can now salute the publishers and editors of the Santa Ana **Register** and all papers like it. Which, despite my put-down hints earlier in this chapter, are more numerous than you might think. As I told you, editors had mothers just as you and I did. They, too, learned eternal verities at mother's knee; they, too, were under the influences of sweet grandmothers and no-nonsense granddaddies. We can love those editors sincerely.

The Text of Paid Advertisements

The public relations director of any church must, of course, be sure that he works with such editors with faithfulness and care. He must have news that is appealing, and write it skillfully for the papers. But he must also cooperate closely with the paper's advertising department.

He himself should write the paid display ads, and indicate the type styles and sizes to be used, along with any illustrations. Again let me warn everybody that kindly Dr. Prototype and his secretary Mary Lu are not likely to be capable of this — yet it is they who, perhaps ninety percent of the time, do take on the responsibility.

Despite his possible Ph. D. and D. D. (Doctor of Divinity), despite his great intellectuality, his brilliance in theology, his knowledge of literature and sociology and psychology, his love of God and of people, dear Dr. Pro probably doesn't know one type face from another. Ask your pastor tomorrow, "What do printers mean when they refer to 'studhorse type'?" He won't know, unless by some rare coincidence he has been much around print shops, that "studhorse" is the slang term for Gothic, a rather ugly type face much too commonly used. Or ask him to name any type face at all, and you'll get the same blank stare that Mary Lu probably will give if you ask her. Any green cub reporter out of journalism school knows type face names; the church office folk don't even know that type faces **have** names.

So then let the church PR man "lay out" the paid advertisements, so that the compositor can set them up in the most attractive and effective manner. In this, the paper's ad staff can be helpful. Such details as borders around ads, use of white space and such, all are technical considerations of importance.

If truth be told, many churches need highly skilled advertising **agency** services for their big ongoing publicity campaigns. But that comes high. When your city-wide group begins to function, that's the time to hire an agency; one church alone can seldom afford such talent. Often, too, the advertising agency skills can be combined with other publicity skills, in firms called Public Relations experts (under many individual names, of course.) The PR director at your own church may well have dual talents such as are found in those big, expensive firms, and within the scope of your church's influence can give you very valuable services at minimum cost.

He can be very helpful, for example, in helping the pastor decide on "catchy" titles for his sermons; or even in choosing sermon themes themselves. Together, pastor and PR expert can explore the congregation's interests and needs; can choose themes and titles that promise to be most helpful, most appealing to the people. Whereupon, the PR man then has something good to discuss in the text of the paid advertisements and in news releases, too. Efficiency in this requires a knowledge of human nature, its reactions and responses, as much as a knowledge of Bible history and teachings.

Forget The Pastor's Picture

Most of those advertisements which I praised in the Santa Ana **Register** were amateurishly done, hence missed much in potential effectiveness. Most were built around a photograph of His Exalted Highness, The Pastor himself. This is a common practice in church ads in all newspapers everywhere. "Dr. John Prototype will deliver the message," the ads say, imitatively rather than creatively. And right there is his picture, showing him with a rather forced, self-conscious smile. Not bad, no. Just not good enough.

It might be okay for, say, Billy Graham's photo to adorn all the advertisements concerning his campaigns. But most pastors are just not that striking and not famous enough in the first place, to make their photos of much value in the paper. This has no bearing on the fact that they are loved, respected, and even talented. We must think here of the over-all come-on and publicity value. Few pastors' photos are drawing cards.

Experiments have shown that a good picture of the church itself has more drawing power than any portrait of the pastor. If a photo of the building is used it should be taken by an expert, and many amateur photographers are experts who can take an "arty" approach, eliminating such distractions as cars, signs, power lines, boxes, dogs, garbage cans, kids, and other irrelevancies. An even better thought may be to have a talented artist produce a strong line drawing of the church. He can glorify the scene a bit, and such a sketch always reproduces better in a newspaper than a photo does.

Any kind of church picture in the paper will etch a wrinkle on the reader's brain, so that when he sees the building from the street, he **recognizes** that church. Something tells him it is important. The printed picture has built an awareness in him, which amounts to a psychic injection. The church, he ought to attend; yes, a man ought to attend church. That looks like a good one.

All in all, then, let the church PR man be a publicist with the printed word. In later chapters we shall explore such media as direct mail, billboards, printed leaflets, radio, television. But, after having launched newspaper publicity, the PR man quickly needs to follow up on the **personal** aspects of publicity, applied at the church itself. This includes "maintenance" ballyhoo, designed to keep the church members continually sold on the grandeurs of their church and its religion. But it also stresses the direct personal outreach to strangers in town, or locals attending worship services for the first time, and persons who hitherto have not known much about church life at all.

So please read on.

Chapter 3

"GOOD MORNING, SIR. MAY I SEW YOU TO A SHEET?"

At this point, every reader should have at least these three points fixed in mind:

A. No matter what millions of people still tend to think, "publicity" is not limited to the printed word, and is not necessarily blasphemous or irreverent or even unrefined.

B. Jesus himself was the best public relations expert the world ever knew, hence we have divine precedent and guidance.

C. Churches today will accomplish little or nothing through newspapers and other printed media if the **personal** touch is missing. Person-to-person contact, such as Jesus used, is for us an imperative follow-up.

Wherefore we come now, Mr. Public Relations Expert, to those famous characters who inhabit — or infest! — virtually every church everywhere, the lay personnel called Greeters and Ushers.

They are seldom honored, because they are seldom very efficient. They are seldom efficient because they are seldom trained, even though their work is exceedingly important. They are all too often just taken for granted; they themselves rarely realize what opportunities they have. So let us now vivisect them, In The Order Of Their Appearance, then give them in-depth clinical study, thus enabling everybody concerned to appreciate their big role in public relations. I shall not be too formal in doing this; I shall simply etch some pictures of real cases and point out some potentials in which that nebulous something called "human interest" is very high. Please remember that I speak from years of experience, plus extensive research done from coast to coast and even abroad.

"Howdja Do."

One Sunday morning not too long ago, my Adele and I visited a church in the throbbing city of Evanston, which culturally almost dominates its mother municipality, Chicago. We walked up about ten stone steps. We went through enormous doors that swung hard at our push; they should of course have been propped open invitingly, for the day was balmy. The vestibule, narthex, entry hall, whatever they called it, was itself larger than many a poor peon home that we have visited in our arid Southwest, in which eight or more people lived. It was, in fact, awesome, as was the entire cathedral. Stately architecture, enriched with many ancient religious symbols carved on ceilings and walls; not garish, as too many Catholic churches are, but with artistic restraint. Graceful arches were like interior steeples straining to touch a roof that seemed to hang from a high ceiling-sky. Tiled floors helped bounce muted echoes around, as if maybe angels or God himself had begun whispering to us. All this, mind you, was merely the entryway.

And was that awesome entry inhabited?

Yes, by a man and a woman. Apparently. At first impression, there was some doubt; those two could have been automatons, models, robots. But no, no, they were human; physically at least. Their eyes moved; flicked from straight-forward focus, to us.

In a flashing brain wave it occurred to me that the man could be the mayor, or the governor of Illinois, or surely the president of a bank. And surely she had to be the haughty head of some national female organization. They dressed and looked their parts. But no, no again, that was unkind of my brain, so I got it in hand and smiled at them.

The male robot bowed stiffly — it seemed to be hinged at the belt — and its mechanical throat uttered, "Howdja do." In synchronized nod of its head, the female number added, "Good morning," apparently to the floor.

Then hands were extended. Warily I took one, squeezed it a bit. There was a slight, automatic reflex, a withdrawal of flab. There were smiles; flashing ones, studied, formal. I didn't quite trust myself to express my feelings; I am a trifle zany at times, need I tell you, and I knew that Adele would be worrying about what my reaction might be. She nudged me on to the next door — quite a trek in itself. It also was closed, and heavy; as I strained to push it open I was reminded of a bank vault.

Inside it, another robot met us.

As with that first one, it was clad in tones of gray. This included what is, or used to be, called a long swallow-tailed frock coat in raincloud drab with pin stripes. It included a formal waistcoat or vest, over a white shirt and a fluffy puffed-out black tie. White gold studs were showing. Also cufflinks with pearls. Down below — spats, with pearl-and-silver buttons.

Do you modern young hepcat readers — including you, Mr. PR man — know what spats are? Or were? Look up the word **spat**. No, it is not an alternative past tense or past participle of **spit,** it is not concerned here with expectoration at all — no matter how I felt! It comes, I seem to recall, from the top-heavy word **spatterdash.** So look that up, kids; doing so will be fun and will Improve Your Minds. You too, pastor.

This erect creature also was hinged at the belt line. Its upper half now leaned forward an inch or two while its eyes continued to stare straight ahead. Then from deep in its mechanical larynx it rumbled — I swear it did — "May I sew you to a sheet?"

Well, no, probably it didn't.

No doubt I was just mind-conditioned by memory of having read, many times, that most famous of all Spoonerisms. The one in which a church usher really did get his tongue tungled and say that to somebody arriving at the door. But he was no worse than the haughty dowager who marched down the church aisle alone and found her accustomed seat already taken by another dame. She lifted her lorgnette and said, "Pardon me, madam, but you are occupewing my pie."

Anyhow, what with Adele furtively elbowing me to keep quiet and behave myself, we got escorted away down yonder by that automaton, whereupon it about-faced in mechanical-military fashion and clacked on back to its station by the inner door. In our pew I bowed my head, stopped grinning, and prayed for my soul. I needed to. I well knew that my Lord has a sense of humor, also a sense of what is right and proper and efficient and friendly and kind. But I wasn't being very reverent as I entered that tabernacle, so now I wanted to make sure that I still ranked acceptably in his good graces.

True, true, my friends, I have exaggerated in the above report.

But not much!

I am afraid that my verbal picture is all too accurate, in showing how thousands of greeters and ushers perform in churches across the United States, Canada, England, Australia, and those nether lands I mentioned. For I have seen them in action; and marveled at them, wondering how in the high hopping hades they could possibly envision themselves as winning friends and influencing people favorably toward their church.

I do not say that to be critical. More properly, the word for them is pitiful. Undoubtedly those servants of God are well-intentioned. It's just that they are hangovers from a drearier era of church mechanics and programming. They Hark Back to a time when stiff formality at church seemed of the uttermost importance. Through a long, **long** stretch of centuries during which almost everybody felt that God was not only awesome but was glowering and vengeful and so severe that he was likely to strike anybody with lightning who dares appear to be **enjoying** church and its worship services.

We still see a lot of that in what we Perfect folk call the heathen religions. Look at those horrible golden gods of Asia, for instance; enormously fat and forbidding idols squatting around glaring and frightening the unholy bejabbers out of mere mortals. Look at the utterly grotesque and hideous black faces of the god portrayals in lands of the savages. Vindictive gods. Mean gods.

Happily, civilization — so called — has lifted most of us occidentals a long way out of that, yet there are still some incidental hangovers of custom, some latent fears. Some of **us** still dare not risk offending God by smiling and being cordial and outgoing, and happy natured and relaxed.

And right here, dearly beloveds, I feel sure that my point once again has been made clear to most of you.

Yet I do want to stress the fact that guiding the greeters and ushers at church, using them to best advantage for the ongoing glory of Christianity (and of other religions as well) can be upgraded tremendously by our hypothetical church employee, the PR expert, the public relations person. He or she will quickly be able to teach those erstwhile robots to stop being mechanized so as to greet us sinners in such hearty though perhaps muted words as "Good morning, sir" and "Hello there, how are you?" and "Susan, and Margaret, how nice to see you!" Love, my friends, is not and never was a glowering fat slob-of-a-god in costly solid gold or even in stone; was never carved hideously from the trunk of a palm tree or a bit of teak. God is love.

Selecting and Training the Greeters

In quick theory, "anybody" can serve efficiently as a greeter at the church door.

In quick fact, the theory is fallacious, and both the pastor and his PR expert must recognize this. In some churches today our Dr. Prototype or his Mary Lu selects the greeters, by telephone. History shows that one couple out of three will **agree** to be greeters next Sunday, and about one out of four of those will either forget the agreement entirely, or ignore it, or will show up late, breathless and embarrassed at finding that half the pews are already filled. In short, the greeting assignments are just not taken seriously.

So then, turn the matter over to your paid PR man. Order him to study the membership personnel and choose greeters who are not only dedicated, dependable worshipers of God, but have also a big plus factor in their knowledge of the social subtleties. They need to have an instinctive feeling for friendliness and cordiality, one that permits no over-effusiveness, no flippancy, but also no stiffness and ridiculous formality.

Because if truth be known, gentlemen and ladies — the greeters and the ushers constitute possibly the most important of the "selling" forces that are operative in the church. The human craving for sociability, for comradeship, friendship, fellowship, call it what you will, is definitely stronger than the craving for "religion." Most of us think we **already are** religious. We say that we do not really need to attend church every Sunday, we can worship under a tree or at the beach or in an airplane or before the fireplace at home. We can indeed — but do we? Yet the realization that we **can**, somehow leads to believe that we **do**, and our consciences are appeased, or at least narcotized. On the other hand, in our gregariousness we will go to any length to find fellowship with people of our kind.

That can well begin right at the church door, when the lukewarm Christian, the potential church member — or even the lethargic member, who has been attending for many months — is given his Sunday morning greeting and is then being escorted to his pew with a quick touch of friendliness.

Exactly How To Greet People At The Church Door

It would astound you to know how many other good-hearted people simply can't think **how** to be efficient greeters at church.

That **modus operandi** would seem to be obvious; a mere matter of common courtesy, of being natural and friendly in easy-going relaxed manner. But studies into this delicate situation show clearly that most haphazardly chosen greeters at the doors of a sanctuary tend to lose their wits. They freeze up with self-consciousness or shyness, they suddenly turn formal, their faces and manner showing strain. Happily, there are many exceptions.

Very few greeters today are like those specimens that Adele and I encountered in Evanston, you may say. I wish that were true. But I repeat — the national stiffness of greeters is appalling.

Surprisingly, geography seems to enter into this. Doubtless you already know about the effect of geographic location on other human functions, actions, and reactions, on customs and costumes, on mores and manners, at least across the vast American land. We worship precedent more than perspicacity. For instance, we all know that what is "right and proper" in right-and-proper Boston is a far cry from what is top-dog in more flambouyant Los Angeles-Hollywood.

Yet it was in staid, proper, Puritanical Boston, not far from where the severe and devout Pilgrims landed, that a lady greeter in a Baptist church kissed me, a stranger, as I entered the door. Shaking hands, she asked, "Where are you from, sir?" When I said Phoenix, Arizona, she impulsively bussed me on the cheek and exclaimed, "I just knew you were from out West! Your deep tan said so. Well I have a daughter living out West myself, and I plan to visit her some day. In Akron, Ohio." Those two cities are, of course, right next door to each other! How wonderful are thy people, dear Lord.

Somewhere between her effusion and the computerized restraint in Evanston, lies the ideal performance which can be a guideline for church greeters everywhere.

How shall you coach those greeters, Mr. PR expert?

First, tell them not to over-dress, as many tend to do. "Come casual," you may want to say. "Or just wear what you would if simply going to a pew yourselves. After all, you are no uniformed doorman, sir, and you madam are not bare-legged bunny-type welcoming people at a theater or night club, hence needing theatrical costuming. You are just one of the congregation, on duty this month. Next month it may be a couple of the very people whom you have greeted."

At which point, research shows, the prospective servant often asks, "But what should I say to the people as they arrive?"

Answer: "Just be yourself. Because this is a church, doesn't mean that friendly greetings must somehow or other be on a higher esoteric plane than any similar welcome in a refined home. Sincere friendliness is your cue. Don't be shy, but don't be too 'forward,' either. **Look each person straight in the eye**, smile and say 'Good morning, it's nice to see you. Please come right in.' Say it with variations, of course; not by memorized rote. Just relax and **enjoy** being a greeter."

As for the Arnold technique — very often, spotting something eye appealing, I say in muted tone, "What a lovely new dress!" or sweater or coat or whatever, as I shake hands. I don't go overboard with it, I just smile and murmur my appreciation. I may say to a man, "Hey, Bill, you are looking great this morning. I like that necktie; it says you have sunshine in your heart." So all right, I am a malarkey merchant, and that approach does indeed often get me an invitation to dinner. Well and good! A more potent fact is — compliments, real ones, are too few and far between for any of us. But remember, all ye greeters and ushers — a compliment is the applause that refreshes. Any person glows inwardly when complimented sincerely. Indeed each of us craves approval all our lives; neglect in expressing it is the saddest of tragedies, certainly in the average home; ask any psychiatrist. In paying my compliments there, I am functioning in a dual role: as a greeter (or usher), and as a public relations man for my church.

When a child comes to the door where Adele and I are greeters (couples function better as greeters than singles do) I stoop or squat low so as to get eyeball-to-eyeball with the mini-sinner. If it's a little girl, I say in low, loving tone, "Hello there, sweetheart. It is so nice to have you come to church. And what a pretty dress you have on!"

So? So I am very popular with the junior female set. And without being in the least hypocritical with it.

If a little boy shows up I also give him special attention from down near his eye level. "Hi there, old timer." Or "Hello, big fellow." (Small boys love to be called big). I smile gently at him, maybe touch his shoulder, his head, his arm. Children feel awkward at shaking hands, so don't try that unless he offers to. Never mind telling him how fast he is growing. Ask him, instead, "Are you having a lot of fun at home and at school?" You've got him! Fun is his metier; **joie de vivre**, enjoyment of life. He probably will nod his head, grin and answer "Yes." Wink knowingly at him and whisper, "Welcome to church. I like you very much." Camaraderie. Love. I am also very popular with the junior **male** set. And do I ever enjoy that!

Those kids tend to be sharper than you and I are. You can't get by with any cheap stuff, can't talk down to them. They are extremely important members or potential members of your church, hence, your public-relations contacts with them should be skilled. This can carry over from Sunday School, right on through worship in the big sanctuary, thence into the patio for social hour. I think of handsome little five-year-old Jeff, who has no grandaddy, hence has sort of latched onto me as a surrogate. Most Sundays he comes into big church with his mommie — and be doggoned if he doesn't have a strange habit of carrying dimes or quarters behind his ears! I know, because with a quick flick of my fingers I find them there, then give them to him to keep. This takes only fifteen seconds or so at the church door, but I have high reputation among the kindergarten set as a master magician. His talk encourages other twerps to test my skills, and little girls seem most interested of all. Probably costs me $100 a year, but I get at least $1,000 worth of publicity and fun out of it, for my church and for myself.

Let the PR expert remember that big John Willinghorse does not make a good greeter at the church door. He is priceless at repairing the furnace and even tinkering the organ pipe that has begun to squeak, but he gets a bit tongue-tied in his social contacts. Love him, but let a somewhat more polished set of individuals or couples do the greeting.

"The Hushers Will Get You"

That they will! If you are a naughty child, sitting with your gang in a pew, and you "act up." And if the hushers are doing their duty.

The hushers — ushers — are **ipso facto** policemen.

No, not the kind that roar around with sirens screaming to arrest bank robbers and muggers; the kind that show people to their seats in church and strive to keep them happy there. But as with the greeters at the door, the ushers must be carefully chosen. Again, it would seem that "anybody" could usher. Anybody has sense enough to walk anybody else down the church aisle and point to an empty pew — right?

No. Anybody can't. Not if your church wants to build subtly strong public relations with its members and any strangers who come in. It is not good enough simply to telephone a few folk **ad lib** and coerce them into ushering next Sunday. Never!

Choose ushers who are outgoing, friendly types; never too nonchalant, never flippant or given to smarty talk, but never stern and dour types either. They need to be down-to-earth and alert, sensible, genuine, and friendly. Which — come to think of it — all of us in all walks of life need to be! You can't just pluck one out of the membership in a casual way; somebody has to **study** the membership personnel, choose a few stand-outs, then train even those. Effective church publicity or public relations depend much on those talented few.

Seek out a happy, relaxed bunch of members to be ushers. Then call meetings and give them stiff briefings in cordial, friendly manner. There is much, **much**, that they don't know, however wise they may be in other areas. In fact, the church membership in general has little real knowledge of what good ushers must learn and do.

In training ushers, start with guidance on how to dress for their jobs. As with greeters, many tend to think that something special is required. Not so. The only criterion is that abiding one for all of us — good taste. And even that varies with individuals, because such factors as age, build, and personality projection, must be considered. But it is unnecessary for the PR person to make much of this in any event; it's the mentality, not the shirt points or the hair do, that counts in an usher. Just dress neatly, without too much flash.

In a great many churches the ushers wear an identifying flower, traditionally a white carnation. This is fine, if the church or the ushers themselves will afford the cost. That flower becomes a badge of office, recognized by the people at large. They know that the carnation wearer is one in nominal authority, able to help not only in finding a seat, but to furnish needed information, or to take charge in any emergency. Sometimes plastic carnations are used, but generally these are regarded as "cheap" and are best avoided.

It helps if each usher has a small name plate on his other lapel. These can be purchased at trivial cost, and kept on file for many uses. Knowing the usher's name builds an intimacy with the people, a person-to-person friendliness and trust.

Rubber heels on ushers are a blessing if the church aisles are uncarpeted, as many are. No usher should ever be heard walking. To a degree, ushers can achieve a non-existent, unrealized omnipresence. If they are carefully trained toward it.

Strangely enough, teen-agers, who normally simply bask in any limelight and tend to crave attention, fit right into that anonymity as silent, unseen ushers. That's because they often lean backward trying to do a Christian service, they quickly become expert at it. (Such a gift may be why young people are forever "taking over the country," to the dismay of us Establishmentarians!) Their main fault, if any, is that they tend to walk too fast as they escort elderly Mrs. Wilberforce Thornapple down the church aisle. Matilda Thornapple has arthritis, and anyway, she likes to look around slowly and see who all is there. Coach your ushers, of whatever age, to let her; to smile gently with her at the people, in relaxed and friendly manner. After all, what is the hurry?

What The Ushers Must Learn To Say

What the usher **says** is important. Actually he is simply a second greeter, hence alertness and cordiality and common sense and love are called for. Tone of voice also is a consideration here. Let the usher's voice always be kept low, because many folk like to bow in prayer when they first sit down in their pews, and because the sanctuary is a holy place in any event. It is not necessary to whisper, but an understandable murmur is considerate.

"Good morning, Mrs. Thornapple; and you, sir. I'm happy to see you. I have excellent seats down front, where you can see and hear everything perfectly. Follow me, please."

Oh dear! That must be a new usher, who doesn't know the Thornapples. Down **front?** In church? ... Horrors!

Wilberforce Thornapple would quickly pay five or ten dollars extra for a front seat at a night club or a theater, for him and his Matilda. But nobody wants to sit down front in church!

Now why don't they?

Studies have been made into this strange, strange quirk of human nature. The distinguished Reverend Dr. George Hunter Hall once said that he was working on an invention. When (and if) he ever got it perfected, he could stand in his pulpit, press a hidden button, and all those rear seats determinedly filled by early arrivals would mechanically be lowered into the basement, then rolled right on down to the front and up to the sanctuary again with the people still in them. Wonderful! He'll make a fortune. Every church will buy one. Meanwhile, all ye good people come early if ye want to get a back seat.

The Ushers' Primary Duty

It is, of course, simply to escort people from the entryway down the aisle to their seats.

Simply? Hah! Many otherwise graceful folk tend suddenly to become very awkward in a church aisle due no doubt to self-consciousness. They strain for dignity, which creates tension and trouble, so they trip over the carpet or toe against heel. I have seen ushers fall flat in church aisles — to their own horror, of course. Also, any one of them can walk much too fast, or much too slowly.

At least half of the typical congregation members develop favorite pews or areas in which they want to sit. The good usher will soon begin to remember those preferences and act accordingly. But lo — very often somebody has with colossal presumption come from out of town and taken one of those favorite places — "Pardon me, madam, but you are occupewing my pie." Years ago, church members could **rent** their pews and hold them exclusively, in certain fashionable churches. The priority feeling still holds in the minds of many, even though it always is ridiculous. In the church where I often am on duty as an usher, we have three general areas in mind — down front, half-way down, and in the rear. "How far down do you prefer?" I sometimes ask an arriving person or party. Almost invariably the answer is "About half-way." The back-row people barge right in and seat themselves, because such pews are very near the doors.

"About half-way" thus fills quickly, so I resort to quick whispered sales talk — "Come on down front, where you can see and hear everything perfectly," then I lead off, and the reluctant ones have no choice but to follow; they do not want to appear discourteous or "make a scene" about it. This sly coercion can fill pews right under the pastor's nose.

A few worshipers very definitely need special seats reserved for them. They are the partially-deaf ones. Until recent years these folk were always stationed down front, where hearing aids were attached to pews. But such aids can work just as effectively in the back row, and often are well back now. Let all ushers be well informed about their locations, and let ushers learn just who is deaf and who isn't. In some churches, especially with many elderly folk, as many as thirty percent may need hearing aids.

Problem Types In Church

Every usher encounters them. And must learn to cope with the more bizarre ones. Typically —

The Spreader. Heaven help us, she is always there! Maybe as many as ten or twenty of her, in a big church. Escorted to an open pew, she lays coat and scarf to her left, Bible and gloves to her right, thereby taking up three potential seats, then bows, prays silently, and self-righteously looks up expectantly for the service to begin. As the sanctuary fills, some usher must perforce smile and silently motion to make room for this couple who have just arrived. She will glare for a moment, as if her rights were being impinged on. But she then will usually pick up her stuff, making quite a production of doing so, hang most of it across her lap, and move over; with frowns of distaste.

The Seat Reserver. In a whisper she tells the usher, "I want to hold these two seats next to me because my friends Bonny and Marguerite may be coming in and looking for me."

Well, phooey, madam, why didn't you three get together outside? The usher doesn't know Bonny and Marguerite. Moreover, while he is seating someone else in another area, some newcomer will hurry in unescorted, spot those two vacant seats and move toward them. A problem! An impasse! Mrs. Hardstone will not "give" an inch; she had told the usher what's what, so let him now defend her rights to hold those two seats. Yes, yes, it is often **Mr.** Hardstone, but generally women are worse seat reservers than men. Moreover, the chances are that Bonny and Marguerite do not show at all, hence, those two needed seats stay vacant all during the service, silently accusing Mrs. Hardstone. She, therefore, gets very little good out of the worship this morning. Which is a sad thing. Ushers are expected to keep everybody happy in church; it is their duty.

The Rigid End-Of-Pew Sitter. He gets there first and by gosh, he is going to sit there or else. He **prefers** the aisle, and has first squatter's rights; let the ushers understand that. Sometimes it is his wife; or both of them, hogging that pew end. If others are shown to that pew, they must climb over the feet of the end sitters.

Sometimes, yes, the end ones will move along and make room. But more often they remain fixed, and the usher is exasperated.

The Stinker . . . Stinker, in a church? What do you mean?

The word is used literally. Sorry to relate, many otherwise gentle and refined persons too seldom bathe, and even more seldom change their underwear. Nicer people just don't want to sit near them. Understandably. Such stinkers quickly get reputations, and there are whisperings to the ushers, who understand, yet must somehow fill that seat next to the offensive person.

Worst offender of all is the smoker. Male or female, this one reeks! Oh no,no, nobody ever smokes right there in the sanctuary. But any smoker of anything — male or female, cigarette, cigar, pipe — carries the offensively stale odor of tobacco smoke around all the time. It permeates the clothing, the hair, even the pores of the skin. Bathing or mouth washings accomplish nothing. One must stop smoking for at least two or three weeks before that nasty odor ends. And in modern society, non-smokers are becoming quite militant, as well they should.

So what can the dedicated usher do about that stinking worshiper who — unaware that he has a foul smell emanating from him — smiles blandly and plops into a pew?

I don't know. If you, my brilliant and hypothetical public relations expert who is training a crew to be good ushers, hence, good publicists, ever find an answer to this question, please write me at once.

Minor Duties Of The Ushers

One routine duty is that of handing out the weekly bulletin called the Order Of Worship. In it is printed the list of hymns, prayer times, sermon topic, litany, responses, everything concerning the morning worship, and usually some bits of church news. (My very small granddaughter calls this the menu).

Such bulletins are best handed out **after** the worshiper has been escorted to the end of a pew, one to each person. The bulletin usually has a picture of the church on its front, or maybe a cross or other religious symbol. The usher should always present it topside up not carelessly upside down so that the worshiper has to twist it around; a small courtesy, worth remembering.

The pastor should work with his ushers in identifying strangers, newcomers, first timers, at each worship service. There are several nice ways to do this. One is — let the pastor ask all strangers to stand, early in the service. Let him then signal his ushers, who come with pretty little blue ribbons of identification to pin on each guest. Later, in the social hour, it becomes easy to greet and "absorb" these welcome newcomers.

I knew at least one big church that gives newcomers not bow ribbons for identifications, but round red buttons on which is printed two significant words —

I'M THIRD

No explanation is given; so the button becomes a conversation opener in the social hour later. I'M THIRD. Can **you**, gentle reader, guess what those words mean, here and now? Think out who is first and second, if you are third. That inexpensive little button becomes a take-home souvenir for the first-timer at church. A sweet touch. Look into that public-relations bit, Mr. PR expert.

As a further minor duty — what does an usher do if, say, the Governor of the State walks in with his family, or a United States Senator with his? Where shall such a dignitary be seated?

Down front, of course; if any seats remain down there. Let the usher not panic. Let him remember that His Excellency is just another humble, God-fearing man who wants no special favors here, no matter what is done for him at Kiwanis Club or at political rallies. Simply say "Good morning, Governor and Mrs. Whoosis. We are honored to have you worship with us. Please come this way." Then seat them wherever you can.

Occasionally there is an exception. One Saturday night in Phoenix, we ushers received emergency alerts that tomorrow morning President Lyndon Johnson would worship with us. All right, we could cope. We helped the Secret Service men search that sanctuary thoroughly in advance of worship hour. No fuss was made, no pageantry prepared. No bombs were found, no lurking assassin. At the appointed hour, one of our ushers quietly waited near the door where our guest would enter.

The president arrived a bit late. But three pews down front had been reserved, roped off with silken cords as per routine there. So the tall, distinguished man silently walked in and was escorted to his pew, just as a town street sweeper might have been. No fuss, no pageantry, no fanfare. The SS men quietly kept him guarded, as always. Mr. Johnson sat down, bowed low in prayer, then sat up to enjoy the choir and the normal service.

At the time for the morning offering, one of our newer ushers drew the area where Mr. Johnson sat. He moved the plate along, slowly. Each SS man dropped in a $5 bill. But Mr. Johnson was bowed low again — he **was** devout, no matter what we revoltin' Republicans and Goldwater fanatics might have thought of him. He did not see that usher with the money plate. The poor usher! He turned pink, but he stuck it out, patiently waiting, pretending to be at ease.

No doubt our President had much to pray about — and don't we all! And to our credit, most of the people bowed with him during his silent prayer; this is "one nation **under God.**" So we did not disturb our President; we joined him.

Then when he straightened his back again he did see the reverently waiting usher holding the plate. Both smiled gently. Mr. Johnson hastily reached for his hip billfold.

The daggoned thing wouldn't come out. Seemed as if the buttonhole was too tight — Lady Bird should have gotten her needle and thread and thimble out before he left home, maybe; or her little scissors. He squirmed, tugged, smiled grimly, with everyone now looking at him and feeling for him, a man with any Common Man's problem. Finally he stood up, reached around and forced the pocket open by popping that stupid button off. He took the billfold out, sat down again, removed six $10 bills, smiled his thank-you to the usher (who will, of course, tell his great-grandchildren about that incident) dropped the money into the plate, folded his arms and looked toward the pulpit as if to say "I'm sorry for the delay, sir; please proceed."

A bronze plaque on the end of that pew today says PRESIDENT LYNDON BAINES JOHNSON WORSHIPED IN THIS PEW ON (DATE). That church may have to be torn down before the year 2000, due to economic and environmental factors, but that pew will be removed into some big new church and in the year 2100, probably even 2500, people will be reading that bronze plaque. May its legend live on!

Publicity Value

Inescapably, that visit by a President became priceless publicity for our church. The word-of-mouth spread everywhere, and is still spread. The newspapers and magazines told the story. The true legend will go on rocking down the ages. Let any public relations man grasp the significance. Celebrities are a part of the ushers' responsibility, and their coming to your church is news. Very few churches can hope for a President to attend. But your local mayor might be there, your governor, your senator. Perhaps Miss Sadie Glutz, the pretty high school baton or pompon cutie who ran away to Hollywood, will return some day as Beautiful Beverly Buxom, the television star, will attend her old hometown church and greet a lot of old timers. This happens quite frequently and the publicity value of it is good both for her and for the church. Do not accuse Sadie — Bev — of being hypocritical; maybe she really does feel the call of God. And who are you to judge, anyway? Look to your own sincerities. Meanwhile, the publicity value to the church swells in proportion to how the ushers and the public relations man "handle" her — figuratively speaking, of course! In our American advertising and publicity campaigns, pretty girls sell everything from shampoo glop to automobiles to European tours to fertilizer to aspirin; often in ways that seem downright ridiculous. But if one or more of them somehow manages to call attention to your church, make the most of that! Advertising — I repeat — is nothing more or less than "calling attention to, and motivating."

Ushers Do Much More Than "Ush"

They are, as I told you, **ipso facto** policemen.

No, no, Junior, not the kind that roar around town arresting outlaws, but the kind that quietly do many good turns and get scant credit for it.

"The hushers will get you" if you misbehave in your pew. Indeed! In fact they must. Because all too frequently little Butch McGillicuddy in his pew with his henchman gets out of hand. Suddenly the adult worshipers, and the nearest usher, will be aware of some giggly, unholy activity created to offset boredom while the pastor builds toward his climax.

So remind your ushers, Mr. PR man and Personnel Manager, that children are children, yes, but are intelligent, too. They must be loved, must be given opportunity to worship with us old cruds in the main sanctuary now and then, but can't often just be turned loose in there. Parents do turn them loose in there, worse luck, while they themselves go on home or somewhere and pick them up at dismissal time. Or even if with parents, Butch and his henchmen, both male and female, can act up so persistently as to distract everybody for six pews around.

Good Dr. Prototype cannot compete with such a performance, so it is up to the ushers to defend him. Police action. Coach the ushers in gentleness, with firmness. If some supersensitive smother-mother adult gets huffy about it — let her. The usher's duty is to the vast majority, who will avidly bless him for doing his job. I remember one "Butch." Never mind his real name. Verily, he was a Dennis the Menace, and I as a sort of grumpy next-door Mr. Wilson, loved him even as I avoided him. One Sunday he was in the rearmost pew of our great cathedral in Phoenix, where the uncarpeted floor under the pews slopes for a figurative half mile down yonder to the chancel area, slopes sharply so that all worshipers can have a good view of pastor and choir. So — Temptation raised its grinning, horned head, and probably also waggled its forked tail. Very young Butch suddenly dropped fifty marbles onto that hardwood floor under his mid-section pew near the rear.

Click-clackety-bang-bump-rattle-and-clatter.

Seemingly, you could have heard those marbles in the next block, speeding down hill, knocking the heels of matrons who shrieked, causing one grand unholy furor.

It was too late, of course, for any preventive police work. But big Charlie Dawson, our head usher, had seen Butch drop those marbles. Smiling benignly like an angel himself — but with a parental glint in his eye (Charlie had five kids of his own) — he quietly, quickly lifted Butch out of his pew and carried him out a side door. In the patio, Butch bit big Charlie on the arm. Which was a mistake, because Charlie then rolled him over and whapped him once, hard, on his boyish bottom. Butch turned sullen, so Charlie carried him on into the church kitchen, sweet-talked him, fed him some of the punch and cookies being prepared for patio use, thereby getting the lad restored to sanity and sense. When Butch's dad heard about the incident later, he shook hands with everybody concerned and in gratitude sent the church a check for $100. Blessed are thy people, O Lord; thy sensible ones, I mean.

News of that incident got around, and we snide members of the church publicity committee slyly did what we could to encourage it. Maybe we were a bit unctuous about that; you know — two-faced. But a subtle half-giggly new atmosphere pervaded, for awhile; the church was not merely a place for prevalently pious platitudes, after all, it was inhabited by **people** — parents, kids, home folk. Neither the ushers nor the PR man can dream up that kind of publicity, it just has to happen. But in one form or another it happens almost every Sunday, and the alert PR folk can take advantage of it and nobody else will ever suspect. I'd bet that God himself rather enjoyed that little episode with Butch. God has a sense of humor, you know; man has one, and he made us in his image — didn't he?

To All Ushers — "Let Nothing You Dismay"

That admonition in the grand old Christmas carol is ideal doctrine for all of us any time. It is inescapable for the ushers if they are to perform well. They must be calm men or women, of prompt good judgment.

If much-loved Old Man Dubose sleeps then snores too loudly in his pew — as he did every Sunday until we had to attend his memorial service — the usher in his aisle will quietly, smilingly nudge him awake. All the people nearby will smilingly show their approval and still not miss a word that Dr. Prototype is saying down yonder in his pulpit. It is a nice bit of routine.

But we all tend to miss some of what Dr. Prototype says. Sleeping or "dozing off" during worship service is not limited to a few old people. It is, in fact, universal. There is something about the human psyche or body chemistry or whatever that responds immediately to quiet and peaceful surroundings such as our sanctuaries offer. Once the high-C soprano has subsided and the last organ notes have ceased sending shock waves through the air — look out! The psychic tension drains out of us as we look expectantly at the pastor. It drains further when he speaks to us in solemn soft-voiced sermon. Often the lights are dimmed, with only a glow around his pulpit. Dutifully we pay attention for five, maybe ten minutes, then his melodious voice tends to become hypnotic, the fatigue of the past week catches up with us and our eyelids droop.

A jillion times I have been there myself. By nature I am an adrenalin kid; I move fast, I am impatient, I want things to move right along and not dilly-dally around. We adrenalinites live more fully and achieve more than the sluggish narcotized types, but we also need frequent short spells of complete rest. We often get them in church in spite of our good intentions.

The preacher knows all this, but there isn't much he can do about it. If he resorts to oratorical shouting and bombast his reputation for deep thinking is shot. So he just lets us doze for a few moments. No, the ushers could not possibly shake all of us awake and alert, they can touch only the loud snorers who disturb persons nearby.

Time was, back when preachers preached for two or three hours every Sunday, they appointed certain sharpshooting ushers — "hushers?" — to stand in strategic locations with long bean shooters in their hands. When Old Man Dubose or little Sissy Wilson or Mrs. McTavish or anybody else seemed asleep — POW! Right on the back of the cranium. You think I'm joking? Not at all. It was a fine old early-American custom, very common, especially in the rural areas. I wish my pastor today would re-instate bean-shooting ushers. Assuredly I would be first to apply for the job. I would ask no salary, rather would I pay for the privilege. What fun!

Other problems also arise. Today when little Linda Bankhead develops a bit of nausea during the sermon, a kindly, understanding usher will quickly lift that sweetie from her pew or her embarrassed mother's lap and rush her into the colder air outside.

As an usher in our high balcony one Easter Sunday, I was leading a uniformed Deputy Sheriff toward a high-level seat. He stooped over to bow to a friend he saw near the aisle. That motion somehow caused his six-shooter to pop out of his belt holster. Oh boy — the pretty but lethal pearl-handled gun went clattering down sixteen steep uncarpeted steps until it came to rest against the balcony rail! No, it did not fire; the safety catch evidently was on. But the poor Deputy turned at least sixteen shades of red and stood there appalled, mouth hanging open.

Now he himself was a policeman, presumably with poise and instant knowledge of what to do in any emergency. But with all the nearby worshipers staring in astonishment, I had to clatter down there, pick up that gun and return it to the Deputy. He ignored the seat I then pointed out; just hurried back to the balcony exit and disappeared, never to be seen in that church again. I couldn't blame him.

In that same big church, as in many another, the ushers keep a stretcher hidden behind the rearmost pew against the wall, for quick use in emergency. In my years of service there we must have used it at least twnety or thirty times. People faint in church. Or have severe cramps. Or strokes. Or dizzy spells. Or heart attacks. Sometimes they die right there — and what better place! No matter what, **somebody** has to cope. Who, but the trained ushers!

If they cope well, they unwittingly develop valuable publicity for their church. If they are trained well, Mr. PR man, they cope well.

They need to know such skills as careful lifting of a human form; and how to administer mouth-to-mouth resuscitation and heart massage; how to handle an epileptic with a sudden violent attack; how to calm any nearby spectators; fast motions, without panicky attitudes.

Unwelcome Guests at Church

You just wouldn't **believe** the true stories that are on record about this. Two drunken cowboys staggered noisily into a sanctuary at Wickenburg, Arizona, where the then nationally-renowned Reverend Dr. Charles S. Poling happened to be in mid-sermon. No ushers stopped them because unaccountably this cowtown church had none. So when the drunks began to whoop and talk loudly, Dr. Poling had forsooth to take charge on his own.

"Hi there, pastor!" one cowpoke yelped. "We come to see you perform some miracles. You do make miracles here, don't you, rev-rund?"

The worshipers were utterly dumfounded, shocked. But my friend Charlie Poling was calmness itself, people told me later.

"Yes, gentlemen," said he from his pulpit. "In God's name we do often manage a few miracles here. And in His name **we also cast out devils!**"

Whereupon he lifted his clerical robe, marched down the chancel steps and up the aisle, grabbed both drunks by an arm, shuffled them to a side door and forcibly ejected them. Hurray! A couple of ranchmen then came to their senses and went out to take further charge of those bums. Small wonder Charlie Poling was immensely popular in that town; if, for nothing else, just doing what trained ushers should have been on the job to do. I have seen drunks escorted out of church in my own towns. The alcoholic is always a very special problem.

Dogs also come to church. I have more than 100 authentic reports about their barging in univited. One came to a funeral, put his paws up on the casket and loudly mourned. Sometimes — as in summer, when sanctuary doors are all open — two pooches will just gallop through, chasing one another in play. One pastor's pooch trailed him all the way from home, into the church and on down the aisle, then stood on hind legs and put paws on the pulpit, tongue wagging, eyes lovingly waiting, wanting to be petted. When a horrified usher plunged down the aisle to do something about that, the poised pastor said loudly, "It's all right, my friends. This fine Irish setter is my companion, Shadrach. We often walk and talk together. We love each other, and church is an ideal place to express love, always. Now lie down, Shad, there's a good boy."

Good dog Shad lay down, scratched himself thoroughly, and went to sleep. Stayed asleep there until the organ burst startled him at the end of the service. At the church door, Shad got more loving handshakes than the pastor did. Undoubtedly God was pleased by it all.

A mama skunk entered an open church door in Texas one summer morning. Just walked in; one of Nature's most beautiful creatures, white stripe against black, plumed tail held gracefully and high, nose sniffing. Here, an usher did take charge. Staying a respectful distance from her, he held up both arms, smiled and said to the people, "Everybody just be very quiet and still, please. There is no danger, even if she comes near you, unless you frighten her. Just go right on with your sermon, pastor."

The pastor did so, but most likely no one remembers much of what he said from that point on. Mrs. Skunk smelt no food, and presently wandered on out again. Bless that usher. Quite a few churches have had to cope with skunks during service. At least one rural church that I know about found Mama Skunk nested with her babies far up under the sanctuary floor for two seasons in a row. The good people had sense enough not to bother them. Skunks generally know better than human beings how to live-and-let-live.

As for that even more famous character, the church mouse — you know, the one that many people are as poor as — he is by no means merely imaginary or legendary. Numerous, and prevalent, are better words for him; or her; or them.

He came up through a hot air register one Sunday morning in Des Moines; skittered up a pew and along the back of it, onto a lady's shoulder thence right up her collar and settled down in her hair. Four people immediately behind her panicked, even though the lady herself hadn't even noticed — which could be held as a tribute to the pastor's gripping sermon!

Screeches of those panicked people brought an usher on the run. But that poor man could see nothing amiss. After all, a mouse is diminutive, easily hidden; and, if it gets to that, completely harmless. While the preacher paused in his sermon and looked wonderingly at his people, the lady involved felt Mickey's motions in her hair. Calmly — surprisingly? — she told the usher where the little creature was, then just waited; some women have better nerves than others. The good usher took out his handkerchief as a shield against getting nipped, quietly grabbed Mickey and escorted him through a door. No harm done, thanks to a calm lady and a calm usher — who unwittingly thereby launched much good free-publicity talk for that church!

Some churches maintain church cats as church-mouse insurance. But then, the cats themselves tend to cause ecclesiastical discombobulation, or something. Mammy cats have kittens — need I tell you. Thomas cats howl, and may do so during worship services conducted by human beings. At least one tabby, whose story came to me, liked to curl up in the organist's lap during Sunday morning services. The organist told the ushers, "Let her be. She is a sweet kitty and she needs to escape from her kittens now and then." Well, don't all mothers? Church folk are a "family," we say, and good cats, as with good dogs, can grace almost any home. Let the ushers go mind their own business.

Details, Details!

Warn your ushers, Mr. PR man, that they must always expect the unexpected, and must handle it properly when it arrives. The people are comforted by the efficiency. Also the people are given to asking endless questions, which the ushers are expected to answer —

"Please," they whisper urgently, "which way are the rest rooms?" That is the most-asked question, probably in all churches ... And, hey hey, **I am reminded of a story!** Another absolutely true one. At our big Community Presbyterian Church in Laguna Beach, California, a stranger came out the front door, caught an usher and asked where to find the rest rooms. That inefficient usher didn't know. But The Reverend Dr. Albert O. Hjerpe happened to overhear, and he did know. Pointing across the north patio, he said, "The women's room is through that hallway to a white door. **But the men just go behind that bush!"**

He was completely truthful. The men did, and still,

go behind a big bush growing there near a cloister. Beyond it is another door with MEN on it.

Ushers hear questions on almost every subject conceivable, from "How much salary does your pastor get?" to "What is your honest definition of God?"

But even having answered questions, the ushers' duties are not ended. Immediately after people have filed out of the sanctuary following the benediction each Sunday, somebody must walk up and down the aisles looking carefully right and left. That's because Miss Conniption Fitz, fondly called Connie, has a habit of leaving her purse under her pew and her sweater hanging on the back of it. Connie is much loved, and makes a generaous pledge every year, and pays it on time, even if she is quick-tempered. So she must not be offended, must in fact be handled with tact. Similarly, people leave their Bibles in their pews, along with scribbled notes, pocket knives (Old Man Weeblefester always allows his to slip out of his pocket) coins, gloves — usually just **one** glove — hats, jewelry, handkerchiefs, lipsticks, scarfs, earrings, fountain pens, toys, this and that on and on **ad lib de luxe,** and if you ask the harrassed ushers, **ad nauseam.**

In most city churches, those forgotten items must be rounded up immediately. That's because gangs of thieves have developed a habit of darting into the church at adjournment time, pretending to be a part of the crowd, then making quick pick-up of any valuables left behind, purses especially. It is not uncommon in a big church for ten or fifteen purses to be left on or under the pews.

IT MUST NOW BE APPARENT TO EVERYBODY that greeters and ushers can literally make or break a church. Theirs are the most effective public relations contacts that the church can have, though hitherto this fact has generally been unrecognized.

Chapter 4

THAT WONDERFUL INSTITUTION, THE COFFEE HOUR

For no known reason the Protestants of America back in the late Reconstruction (Victorian) Era and in the Teddy Rooseveltian decade, slipped into the feeling that 11 a.m. was the **only** hour at which to begin Sunday worship at church. Thus they adjourned about noon, shook the pastor's hand, and hurried home to their midday meals.

Their friends, the Catholics, had long been having Mass several times each Sunday morning, with little time between. Generally they still do. I remember once not long ago having a hotel room directly across the plaza from a stately cathedral that served a town in our Mexican Southwest. Be doggoned if that cathedral didn't have a tower bell that knocked me out of bed at 5:30 every morning! It **bong-gonged** bigger than Big Ben in London, calling the faithful to six o'clock Mass. I remember I got mad for two mornings. Then on the third day, awake anyhow, I got up and went to Mass myself — protesting Protestant that I was. Nothing happened; about my being a Protestant. Well, yes it did, too. The good priest recognized me as a stranger, learned that I was a Presbyterian, and invited me to breakfast. What a doll of a person he was, and I suppose still is. I chewed him out for waking me so early. You should have heard him laugh! He said, "Mr. Arnold, we Catholics have been trying to awaken you Protestants for centuries!" How can you not love a sweet guy like that?

But even the Catholics did not — and often still do not — allocate any time for sociability after Mass, any refreshments and chitchat and all that. Make-ready has to be done for the immediate **next** Mass; people filing out, ushers policing the pews, priests generally relaxing for a few precious moments, the organist and singer ditto. So, mostly, The People just go home.

Today, however, eleven o'clock is no longer exclusively sacred for us. Many, many Protestant churches have services as early as 8:30, then again at ten. Some have them at 9 and 10:30. Quite a few have **three** Sunday morning services. A few, notably in rural areas, have afternoon worship. Not many churches still try to hold regular preaching-meeting at night, as was the custom prior to 1940 or so. Go to church on Sunday **night?** Heavens, we today would miss our favorite program on TV! No way! First things first. I can just hear the family howling in horror. Which change — come to think on it — may not be as sad as it sounds. Horrid though it is much of the time, television has much, much to recommend it, and parent-child togetherness in the living room could be better than forced piety in the sanctuary. Times have changed, and I think for the better. The morning church routine has changed for the better, too. Among other grand improvements for both Protestants and Catholics, and also for the Jewish people at their synagogues, has been the development to near perfection of what is, regrettably, called The Coffee Hour. It should have a better name.

With services or Masses stringing along in close sequence, those folk coming **out** of the pews now go to a special place where their noise will not disturb worship in the next service or Mass, and fraternize socially for a time.

It has become one of the happiest facets of life in North America. Truly, The Coffee Hour has become a national institution, a social phenomenon.

In The "Olden" Days

Back yonder when grandpappy was a kid — he will tell you now if you give him half a chance — quite a few church families took baskets of food and had complete meals after services ended. In fact for many decades "dinner on the grounds" was an institution in the rural churches of America; not every Sunday, but maybe every quarter at least. People would eat, visit, then all pitch in and work. Men would clean the adjacent cemetery of weeds and trash, repair fences and other exterior properties. Women would sweep and dust and "slick up" the inside of the building, and maybe even the parsonage if it were close by, as it often was. Love, not duty, motivated those ancestors of ours. Some of us moderns perform similarly; for in recent months I have been on a work crew at my own church; after dinner in the patio. An American custom; a holdover from farm folk, ranch folk, small-town folk, village folk, before urban sprawl was invented.

We do not know who invented "The Coffee Hour" as we know it today. Probably it just slowly evolved, and spread until it has become a revered routine. Is it important? Keep this unquestionable fact in mind: **for millions of humble folk, in thousands of churches, that coffee hour is the highlight of the week, all year long.** These have few if any other social outlets whatsoever. It is indeed pathetic to see how little contact many fine people have with other people. And so, you ask me if The Coffee Hour is important! Truth is, its importance at church and in the lives of its members is now held to be almost as great as the worship service in the sanctuary.

"Ought To" Changed To "Want To"

One summation is — The Coffee Hour has taken some of the "ought to" out of church attendance, replacing it with an enthusiastic "want to." And **that** is because almost all of us are basically lonely, much of the time. We have disappointments in the people we encounter on weekdays, maybe; even among our own family members, too often. But at church, somehow the people have been screened; we just know that those in the patio are good-hearted, friendly, kind. We are gregarious by nature, and, of course, prefer to be with people we can like and trust. Where else in all our routine of living, can we be more sure of finding them than at church? Sophistication? Phooey on that! "Night club" life, and all that it connotes, is and always was zero in effective rewarding social contacts; it is too patently spurious or "phony" and costly to boot. But we sense that God is in the patio with us, and God is love. So we the church people are now well along toward making the most of The Coffee Hour.

In point of fact, there is plenty of evidence that the church "coffee hour" is as old as Christianity itself, probably older. The good people in Jesus' time foregathered to sing and hear him preach, then sit around visiting while they had refreshments. Coffee probably was not known. But tea, maybe? Or something comparable to our punch? They had citrus and other fruits, and honey for sweetening. And yes, the preacher would then have been "mingling," as in our modern time. And, no doubt, up would come Mr. Iscariot, billygoat beard pointing outward and bobbing militantly as he said to the preacher, "I disagree with what you said about money in your sermon. We have to have bread to eat and that costs money. What with the bureaucrats in government taxing us more and more, we are forced to get money any way we can!"

"I'm afraid you misunderstood me, Mr. Iscariot, sir. When I said that man does not live by bread alone, I meant —"

But Mrs. Iscariot interrupted. "Judas, you let the young rabbi alone, you hear me? He is smarter than you are, I vow. Sir, may I bring you another cup of tea? And some almond cookies, made with fresh, rich camel's milk? And some of those fine Khalasa dates?"

You know how such scenes go, in our modern church social hours. Human nature has not changed much in 2000 years. Our refreshment committees often mis-guess on how many people will be there. Similar mis-guesses were made back there, I seem to recall. Once the crowd was much larger than anticipated, and they ran out of food. But a boy happened to have a couple of fishes, and a few loaves of homemade bread, so the preacher took that little supply, and lo and behold — five thousand people ate at **that** Coffee Hour. They wanted to be there; wanted to, mind you. Which is a significant fact to remember, even about the people at our own social gatherings.

Yes, we often argue with the preacher, just as we imagine was done back there. And yes, he gently tries to explain, tries to get his point through our thick heads. But mostly the time passes in happy talk and togetherness, that matchless intangible called fellowship. Truly it is wonderful just to walk by our Downtown Church of the Chimes (several real churches are named that, incidentally) and see one hundred, two hundred, six hundred people milling about under the trees or in the open court there, chatting and laughing and congratulating the preacher on his sermon and admiring the new babies and making a date with somebody to play golf tomorrow and how is your dear mother who was ill and wasn't the service fine this morning and what a lovely new outfit you are wearing and why don't you two come to our house for dinner tomorrow night and no I don't think the President in Washington knows what he is doing and yes we really do need rain and no you haven't told me your newest funny joke go ahead and tell it. Fellowship! Happy time! Small wonder the Coffee Hour has come into major importance. It is psychologically **right!** It is a priceless supportive portion of the church's ongoing effort to serve our Lord by serving humanity.

But this book is supposed to be about holy ballyhoo, isn't it? About publicity or public relations for the churches?

It is indeed.

And Broth-er, if you can show me a better way to develop happily contagious public relations than maintaining a happy Coffee Hour after service, I will dismiss the meeting here and **you** can take charge.

Word-Of-Mouth Enthusiasm

The wonderful "publicity" fact is — people look forward to that Coffee Hour. All week they talk about it with neighbors and other persons, in direct contact and frequently by telephone. Bits of news are passed along — the preacher's pretty young wife is going to have a baby, the sexton had a heart flare-up again, and on and on, all week.

Yes, we also have a strong heart yearning to worship God, so we do go into the sanctuary, and would go if there were no Coffee Hour. But our enthusiasm for the over-all relationship to our church would not be nearly so high. It is important — indeed it is vital — that we associate with good people in direct person-to-person rapport. You cannot associate with other people of any kind without acquiring some of their characteristics, their attitudes. This begins with prayer inside the sanctuary, and carries right on out into the Coffee Hour, during which we shake some hands and clap some backs and hug some people and even kiss quite a few of the very old, the very young, and the very pretty.

The public relations man (or woman) hired by your church must latch onto those facts and exploit them to the fullest. It does no good to publicize or advertise a "product" if it isn't there for delivery when the customers come.

No, it is not necessary to create a Sunday "bingo" party effect, ever. (Literal bingo, the game, is indeed used as a money-raising come-on by many Catholic and some Protestant churches. But it is quite definitely in poor taste and ill repute, a tacit endorsement of gambling). All the PR person need do is encourage the goodness of the Coffee Hour, the gentility, the sweetness, the brotherly love, the restfulness, the pervading peace of mind. The better this Coffee Hour is, the most the news of it will be spread by the people. Sinners always are lonely, lonely persons, even though they associate with other folk all the time. They themselves know that. So the appeal of the happy visiting, along with spiritual inspiration acquired in the sanctuary, can be very appealing and healing, and this Good News quickly gets around. Neighbor tells neighbor. Worker tells worker. Child tells child — and let no Coffee Hour managers dare neglect the children! This is not a studied campaign of propaganda, it simply happens in incidental conversation during weekdays and nights. Word of mouth — the most effective "publicity" in the world.

First Cue For The Public Relations Man

His (her) first task, regarding the Coffee Hour, is to upgrade it.

Despite its merits, it is not yet perfect. Perfection is an "impossible dream" for almost anything any time, a rainbow whose pot of gold we never quite reach before the bow fades. Yet we all pursue it. We must! Or life is without motivation and purpose. And realistically, our Coffee Hours are still quite down scale, considering their grand possibilities.

To begin with, literal coffee is not all that important, and should be relegated to the secondary position it deserves. Take some recognition of us militant screwballs who will settle for a de-caff concoction, or who would really much rather have tea. Keep in mind that "everybody" does **not** want coffee, no matter what the caffein addicts claim. And — the children? Punch, then.

Many churches quietly station a ''chipping-in bowl'' on a table somewhere near the exit from the patio,* and good-hearted people always take the hint. I have seen five-dollar bills turn up in there, along with many dollar bills, so that such bowls almost always turn up a profit for the Refreshment Committee, which then can upgrade everything that is served, and without feeling pinched.

Cookies also are important. Cookies just seem to belong wherever those drinks are served. But again, be sure they are of high quality. Make a deal with some of the church women loners, the widows or others alone: **pay** them to make delicious fresh cookies each Saturday. You will be doing them and everybody else a favor. By all means avoid those overly-advertised things in plastic or other containers at grocery stores. They taste like pasteboard, and usually are as stale as last Sunday's jokes.

Yes, you'd think all these details would be self-evident, would be so obvious as to need no recording here. But actually, they are either unknown or are flagrantly ignored in churches all across the continent. In fact I often marvel at the manner in which otherwise discriminating and well-to-do folk, who demand and get high quality living in their homes, feel that **cheapness** is acceptable at church! These folk will eat expensive roast beef for supper at home, then bring a skimpy casserole or a padded meatloaf to the church dinner, at which the mother will dine with the same guests she had in her home dining room. Why? Don't ask me, I only work here; and get mad about such inconsistencies. But don't **you** get mad, Mr. PR man; you are paid to be both diplomatic and emphatic when serving the church. Just as the pastor is.

*Translate patio to your own local situation.

Hosts and Hostesses

If, say, 200 people stream out of the sanctuary and into the parlor or patio or Coffee Hour, you can be sure that about 129 of them are a little bit shy. They are reluctant to barge right up and demand quick service with their coffee, tea, punch, or cookies. They stand back. They wait, smiling, pretending not to be eager.

These are all loveable, valuable patrons of the church, and it is **somebody's** duty to take charge of them.

Good Dr. Prototype can't do it. Invariably, he is still up yonder at the narthex or vestibule door, trying tactfully to get Mrs. Sylvester (ClaraBelle) Weems to move along and not hold up the exit line by telling him about her grandchildren or arguing a point in the sermon. It will be maybe twenty minutes before he can get down. And even there, people latch onto him. He may get no coffee or tea at all; may find little opportunity to "mingle" in relaxed fashion and just be one of the relaxed, happy folk there, much less be a host.

Well then, his wife?

Not she! That poor woman is already "put upon"

in two dozen different ways, as you well know if you stop to think about it.

The assistant pastors? They face the same latch-on enthusiasts that Dr. Prototype faces, and must be patient, tactful, loving, kind.

WHO, then?

In advance, let the PR director quietly take charge.

Let him huddle with Mary Lu, the good church secretary, screening the membership directory and listing say twenty names of women and/or men known to be outgoing, friendly, self-assured but not "forward" types. Let him quietly call these twenty together — and happily enlist them for the highly pleasant duty of being hosts at Coffee Hour.

Again, common sense dictates. It is not necessary for any detailed **modus operandi** to be spelled out here. Eight or ten such persons, carefully selected, mutually trained at once-a-month meetings in private, can tactfully steer the shy ones up to the ladies who are pouring the beverages.

They themselves can smile and chat with the **very** shy, can introduce newcomers to old timers, can go rescue the pastor from Clara Belle Weems, who has followed him into the coffee hour, can then present him to newcomers, then re-rescue him when need arises again. Oh, boy, what quiet fun all that is! My Adele and I have been on many such unnamed committees. Serving there is an exalting experience.

And as the PR director well knows, it is a priceless, costless aspect of public relations for any church. The psychological impact of "The Coffee Hour" sometimes seems equal to or greater than the pull of the talented ushers, in bringing people in to worship service, helping them find a closeness with God in person-to-person fashion. I am the church, you are the church, we are the church together. Coffee Hour can help dispel the gloom-and-doom attitude which too many people still tend to hold, instead of enjoying the Good News, the inspiriting qualities of our religion.

Chapter 5

THE ALL-IMPORTANT SUNDAY BULLETIN

Whenever you walk into the great sanctuary of the church to which my Adele and I belong in Laguna Beach, California, — or into the even larger one in Phoenix where we belonged for 44 years and where we still worship in winter — somebody at the door hands you a small work of art.

It is a color picture of the church itself, size 5½ by 8½ inches, that "bleeds" off all four sides (meaning, it has no border framing). The one in Phoenix shows the front steps and doorway with its magnificent carvings above, the tower that is a stately thing of rare grace and beauty, a part of Norton Chapel far across the spacious patio with its arched cloister, seven tall **Washington filifera** palm trees, all against the remarkable turquoise sky that is characteristic of the desert Southwest. It is a perpendicular photograph, composed to emphasize the tower with lighted cross.

In Laguna Beach the same size photograph is also full bleed, but is horizontal. It shows a church very similar in architectural style; a high and graceful tower, parts of two patios or courts with cloister arches, red tile roofs on sanctuary and wings of the building that extend for a full block. The world's most picturesque trees, eucalyptus, very tall and lacey and graceful with their sleek pink-white trunks, are a framing for the majestic tower there. Other trees and shrubs show, and in the foreground, near the camera, is a spread of red geranium blossoms that give the picture a bit of three-dimensional effect.

Each of those photographs is breathtaking in beauty — and you think photography is not an art! The colors are balanced better than those in most paintings. The composition is superb. There are no distracting touches such as cars, trash cans, signs, posing people. The printing is done by perfect offset lithography, which today can make any photograph seem to come alive.

Those photographs were made by experts. I do not know who made the one in Phoenix; it was taken more than twenty years ago. But the one in Laguna Beach I do know about. It was taken recently, on a 35-mm. Kodacolor negative. This photographer was a man with much professional experience, having taken many color photos to illustrate his own articles in such high-level journals as The Saturday Evening Post, Collier's Magazine, Better Homes and Gardens, Holiday, and others — me.

Those strict editors had taught me some know-how. I also had competent help in Laguna Beach; a good friend and fellow church member, the town's leading pharmacist, Charles "Chuck" McCalla. Together we watched for opportunity; just the right position of the sun to strengthen the color of the sky and give the most artistic slant to the tree shadows, no traffic, no parked cars, nothing unsightly anywhere. We took twenty negatives, studied the resultant twenty prints, chose one and had it enlarged to 11 by 14 inches. We took that to the lithographer. When he saw it, his face lit up and he exclaimed in awed appreciation — "WOW!" It was high tribute. It was the reaction we wanted.

Because that also was the reaction we wanted from the worshipers attending our church, who for years would be given copies of the lithographed beauty at the church door. We got it. And we do indeed still get it, from every first-timer. The picture is not only "suitable for framing," it is very often framed and kept in homes or presented as gifts, because it is just that arrestingly lovely.

Why?

I have presented all those details for a purpose. This book is a stated Guide To Effective Publicity For Your Church. And that photograph, presented to every person who enters on Sunday morning, is probably **the most effective item of printed publicity that those grand churches have ever used.**

Understand, this is not theoretical; it is a tested, proven fact.

No. Phoenix and Laguna Beach have no monopoly on such beautiful photos; quite a few other churches have used the same idea. Many thousands more have not, but could, and should.

Let the PR person be sure to get a trained photographer. At least 99 percent of all photographs taken around the world are sheer junk; glanced at once, filed in a drawer or cheap album, then forgotten — justifiably. But the few good ones can bring a genuine lift to the spirit each time they are seen. They are much more than merely a pleasing combination of smiles, colors, and forms, they say something to the viewer, they connote Importance and Worth.

Those lovely church views say to the people — "Here is your local headquarters for Christian fellowship, peace, and love. Make the most of it."

The church publicity department must not make the mistake of merely "going outside and taking a snapshot" of the building. Good equipment, ample time, and a sensitivity for beauty, are absolutely imperative.

Once a fine photo of the church is chosen, do not clutter that full-bleed reproduction with any words. At the bottom of Page 4 of the folder, litho only the name and address of the church, in bold blue letters. Omit names of pastors, secretaries and such, also telephone numbers, because these can be changed at any time thus making your listings obsolete; add such details later, when each week's information is put on with letterpress printing.

Avoid Cheapness

Many churches do **not** hand out a beautiful color photo of the building to people arriving on Sunday mornings at the sanctuary door. Some tend to print those leaflet covers with nothing but a large-type name of the church, maybe its address, and a list of the pastors with their impressive degrees. Often a rather uninteresting black-and-white photo, or line drawing, of the church, is shown in small size. This front page has close to zero eye appeal and value as publicity.

Still other front pages show only religious symbols; crosses, bells, stars, towers, scrolls, kneeling figures, on and on. There is nothing wrong with religious symbols, of course. But in this usage, there is nothing much good about them, either. Tests show that the worshipers receiving bulletins so ornamented scarcely see the symbols at all; there is no real impact. The printed piece is rarely taken home, whereas those beautifully designed ones usually are.

Once more — I feel sure that my point is quite clear.

But for emphasis, let me state it anyway: **church publicity must be of high order; we cannot afford anything but the best.** If the best costs a little more, pay for it; then you can confidently expect encouraging, even exciting results. If and when 3-D color lithography is perfected and offered at reasonable cost, let our churches be among the first to use it.

The "Order Of Worship"

Those bleed litho pictures are the covers of little folders — four or six or more pages — that present the morning order of worship in the sanctuary, including words of hymns, litanies, special prayers, choir renditions, sermon topic, whatever will make the worship program run smoothly.

Preparing the text matter to be printed in that section would seem to be a trivial matter, and indeed it generally is so regarded. Typically, it is originated in part by our old friend Dr. Prototype, shunted to Mary Lu, who hastily telephones the choir director then does what has been done: she makes this Sunday's "menu" just like last Sunday's. Do you, just here, tend to shrug? And say that after all, does it matter? Just so we the people can know what's going on; know when to stand up, when to sit down, when to pray, when to read the responses, generally keep track of things.

But that is a defeatist attitude, Mr. PR man. Doing what has been done. Making that leaflet precedential instead of providential. Dismissing it from mind. Taking it lightly.

Let me repeat — **the very essence of showmanship is surprise.** If your pastor and his secretary don't have sense enough to know that and inject some change, some newness every Sunday, then you take over the job and do it for them. That **is** a part of your job. Week in week out sameness in many aspects of church programming is what has held the churches back more than any other factor. Thousands of churches today still operate almost exactly as they did prior to 1940 or so, whereas the rest of human society has picked up newness and freshness at jet speed.

Exactly how you shall word that Order Of Worship, must be determined in and for each church; I cannot dictate it here. Clarity, for quick-look reading, is your cue. Typeface should be fairly large, lines should not be crowded, extra space should show between units, titles of songs should be in bold italics, title of sermon in capital letters.

It is well to start at the very top of the first inside page with a gentle reminder something like this:

Many people like to bow in prayer immediately after entering their pews. You are invited to join them.

That is a hint to the heedless; to the brash ones who seem to think a worship service is a social event for chatting and laughing and "visiting" ad lib. Thus your leaflet may set the atmosphere for persons who are not quite up to par in dignity and refinement.

At intervals during the first half of that page, insert this line : (Ushers may seat late arrivals.) Again that is a gentle but valuable reprimand; for those souls who habitually barge in some minutes after the Processional or opening prayer. Seating them **during** any song or prayer is always an abomination. So, let the ushers be trained to take a firm stance on this, and whisper to late comers, "Please wait just a few minutes, then we can seat you." Those who did arrive on time deserve and will appreciate that important courtesy, just as they do at the efficiently managed operas or symphony concerts. Which makes it important public relations.

Most of those leaflets — commonly called Bulletins — have a minimum of four pages, made from a standard sized sheet of paper, 8½ by 11 inches, folded once horizontally. Sometimes the dimensions are 9 by 12, rarely larger. The PR man should coordinate this with the printer or the church's own printing equipment, for maximum convenience and minimum cost. Those exquisite color photos — which are the eye catchers, the come-on or theater marquee as people say — are lithographed in quantity in advance; 20,000 to 50,000 copies at a time, for minimum unit expense. They are best stored in the churches, with each week's needed quantity sent to a nearby printer for adding that specific week's material.

This second printing should, preferably, be done by a "real" printer, using either letterpress or litho. But modern office equipment also offers some very attractive opportunities, at less cost, and this should be investigated by the PR man. One hit — the typical roller type hand-operated machine that prints from typewritten composition on a gelatinous sheet or on a special kind of blue paper, is a poor thing at best, and is long outmoded. Results from it look "Cheap." The bulletin so printed looks indistinct, messy, smeary; is in fact quite out of keeping with the high-level thinking that must be associated with all aspects of your church.

Other Text Matter

The literal Order Of Worship itself usually takes up no more than one page, but on occasions may run as much as two pages. That means considerable space is left, even on a four-page folder with all of the front page taken up by that color photograph. So what do you put on that remaining space?

There is never enough of it! If there is, somebody has been loafing, goofing off on the job, as the kids say.

Ask any efficient Mary Lu. Dr. Prototype hounds her to "put this in, please" every Tuesday, because he keeps having good thoughts. But Mary Lu's temper is likely to flare because **she** knows that those lithographed blanks are not elastic, and she already has too much stuff. The choir director has been harassing her also, not to mention the assistant pastor and the Superintendent of Sunday School.

So, let the PR person — who, remember, is a diplomat — sweet-talk Mary Lu. She is a girl; a woman; a female; sensitive but eager and kind. All that the PR person needs to do is laugh a little and tell her she has on a cute new sweater this morning and stop dithering, kiddo, because we will print you an insert sheet of two or four pages or as many as you need, and how about a cup of coffee with me right now.

One single half-sheet insert often is enough to add. But more often, in a big church, it isn't. Dr. Prototype has a compulsion; he must, perforce, sermonize in print, feels that he must adorn that weekly bulletin with a "Pastoral Message." And invariably it is too dull and too long and out of place anyway because he will be delivering a Pastoral Message from his pulpit. Furthermore, very few pastors can write a good sermon in any event; that is true of most expert public speakers. The spoken word and the written word are two vastly different techniques. No pastor, ever, should write out his Sunday sermon then **read** it to his people — horrors! Invariably it will be tediously dull. Let him make a few notes, maybe, but mostly he must get himself revved up and speak out forthrightly from his heart. How the man says it, often is more important for emotional impact than what he says. Literary excellence, scholarly polysyllabification forgivethebigword, must give way to dedicated sincerety from the man's deep psyche or somewhere. Coach him in that, Mr. PR man; never let him **read** a dull discourse in his pulpit.

To that end, take Dr. Prototype out for coffee, along with sweet Mary Lu, and josh him gently while joshing her. The atmosphere will thus become magnolious for all. (That's a Southern idiom.)

Throw out the Pastoral Message, then, and make room for much **church news.**

It is customary, and wise, to print a list of church and Sunday School activities upcoming for the week. Make the wording of those not too flippant, but somewhat chatty and friendly and enthusiastic, not formal. That list itself may cover two pages of the Bulletin — and if it doesn't in your church, maybe your church had better "get with it" and develop more activities. Or its public relations will indeed sag.

So, then, a four-page insert; a second 8½ by 11 sheet, printed then folded horizontally in the center. This need not be stapled into the picture cover sheet, although that helps. In either event, invite elderly Hermina Pierce to drop by the church on Friday afternoons and insert them, for use by the ushers. Hermina is age 86 and is a doll, a sprightly lady whom everybody teases and honors, a widow whom God blessed with adaptability. Incidentally, that is her real name, and she really does those inserts each Friday at our church in Laguna Beach, California, as one of her many contributions. She happily calls herself "the den mother of the church staff," and even our handsome young head pastor is a bit awed by her magnificent and gentle heart.

Almost every church congregation has a Hermina, often several of them; wonderful souls who inevitably are rather lonely. The wise PR person will draft at least one of them, in rotation if need be, as his chief advisor and assistant. That choosing of itself gets talked about, hence becomes good public relations.

What Kind of News? ... Good!

On that added Bulletin space, print short paragraphs of church news.

What kind? GOOD news. Yes, do announce any deaths and funerals, but with fewest possible words; no eulogies here. Do announce that the distinguished attorney, Habeus Korpus, and his wife Alluria who teaches the Junior Saints Sunday School class, have just returned from a grand trip to Hawaii. And that Habeus and Alluria will present their color slides at next Friday night's big Congregational Dinner. (There is no way to avoid letting them show those cotton-pickin' slides! Unfortunately, the Korpuses **offered.**)

Do print that Dr. Bill Zarhigh has been elected President of the State Medical Association, which is deeply concerned with malpractice suits and other problems, and the church extends him congratulations.

Do print this (a real instance; real names): "Those four exquisite little white baskets, filled with rosebuds, that adorn our altar table today in lieu of the usual huge floral display, were given by Linda and Bill Higgs, one of our congregation's most honored young couples. Each basket represents a little daughter, and was placed there in symbolic thanks to God for a beloved child. Our entire church staff and membership join Linda and Bill in their feeling of gratitude." (Oh boy, did **that** ever become good publicity for our church! Got talked about all over town for weeks.)

Do print that people are now using the church's Dial-A-Prayer telephone service at such a rate that two more telephones have had to be added. Explain that new prayers are recorded by one of the ministers each morning, and that anybody anywhere may dial the following number, any time of night or day, and hear a prayer that is sure to be helpful. Keep that Dial-A-Prayer number as a standing line in every week's Bulletin.

Do print that the Junior High Fellowship members will meet in the patio next Saturday at 8 a.m. to go on an all-day picnic at Skyline Point in Superstition Mountain, from which the young people will search for the fabulous Lost Dutchman Gold Mine. Add that all gold found will, of course, be turned over to the church. (None has ever been found up there yet, but — who knows what the future may bring?) Yes, PR person, brighten your news with the heartening, the romantic, the glamorous; and with frequent bits of humor.

Scout for such items, Mr. PR man. There is no end to the possibilities. Conscript several reporters to help you on this Bulletin, and on the church's monthly News Letter (which will be discussed later.) Such helpers will be flattered, and will require no pay. Let them ring a lot of telephone bells, inquiring. Teach them to carry a small notebook, so as to get facts and dates, and by all means get names spelled correctly. At least 99 percent of all the people on earth never, never "get their names in the paper" or in print anywhere else, so if you can manage to print a lot of them in your church publications, good will is certain to burgeon. Of course, that Bulletin **must** be limited; you don't want worshipers forgetting to worship because they have a big newspaper to read in their pews! So for that use, be very selective and brief. Then follow up with a grand newspaper each month.

Properly "thought out," designed, and printed, that Sunday Bulletin — which so often is a "nothing" thing because it is so carelessly done — can become the most valuable single piece of publicity that any church can have.

Chapter 6

THE MONTHLY "CHURCH NEWS LETTER"

Almost literally every church everywhere has one.

In small, impecunious parishes, notably the rural or village flocks, the monthly letter usually is just handed out at the door. Which is okay, because such churches tend to have very high member attendance records, ranging well above 95 percent, perhaps because there is relatively little competition on Sundays in the form of entertainment, but I like to think more likely because country folk just naturally have an edge on us fancy urbanites. I told you — I was born and reared Away Back Of Beyond, in the piney woods. I am proud of it. Jesus himself, you know, wasn't born in a penthouse just off Times Square.

In the sleek towns and cities, the monthly letter usually is mailed, so as to be sure that it reaches the homes of lukewarm members who seldom attend worship services. That letter gives those lip-service people at least a small contact with the church they profess to support.

Generally in America, the monthly church news letter is excellent. It is better than you might guess, considering the absence of professional news gathering, writing, and editing. But even so, Mr. PR man, almost invariably there is room for vast improvement.

Probably I have studied at least a thousand such letters, and I have two very typical ones before me as I write this. One is made of six typewriter pages folded horizontally in the center like those Sunday Bulletins, stapled together on the fold, thus making twenty-four booklike pages. All the printing was done by one of those roller machines, from text typewritten on a gelatinous sheet, in the church office, by Mary Lu herself. The imprint is smudgy, smeary, low in eye appeal yet fairly legible. The paper sheets are mixed pink and yellow, obviously chosen for economy. Thus the total effect is somewhat like that of a circus sideshow advertising leaflet, or like an announcement of a whiskey sale with "Prices Slashed."

The text matter on that letter is not bad, yet is far from tops in quality. It is legible, but uninteresting. It begins with that ubiquitous "Message From The Pastor," who may be a good speaker but is a poor writer, given to unctuous statements and trite phrases. Much of the next two pages is taken up by a statistical appeal for missionary funds. Again — not "bad;" we must indeed send money to foreign lands to help less fortunate peoples. America has only six percent of the world's population, but fifty percent of the world's income. But those and other poorly-printed figures do not "get through" to me, do not really touch my heart. The appeal is ought-to rather than want-to. No emotions are likely to be stirred in those reading it.

Other pages tabulate forthcoming dates of church dinners, outings and such, tell of two deaths and funerals, then end with half a page of "Personals." **Mr. and Mrs. Leland Klingfelter have returned from their vacation in Alabama. They report a good time . . . Marcia Prototype had the High School "Squires" to a party in the manse, AT WHICH HER FATHER GAVE THE DEVOTIONAL.** Again — big deal! Can't you just see the teen-age readers being thrilled at such news, presented with such felicity of expression? I know, I know, I am sounding supercilious and snooty here. But dang it all, that news letter should have had zip and tang and come-on and charm and a lot of talk-about quotability. With just a little guidance from the Church PR person, it could have. It could move from dullness into effectiveness.

The second specimen before me is much better.

It is eight pages 9 by 12 inches in size, high quality white paper printed in offset lithography, three columns to a page, stapled together at the center. It has nine photographs, perfectly reproduced. Yes, there is a "Pastoral Message" here too, but it is rather subdued, with a smiling inset photo of the pastor, all on page 3 — a nice bit, especially for any shut-ins who cannot attend church, and for people who just don't attend often but still do have a "feeling" for their church.

The remaining text is varied, under smallish, well-handled headlines in the daily newspaper fashion. Basketball — two teams in the city church league — table tennis, roller skating, square dancing, and many other activities, have short "write ups' plus a few photos. The personal and family news bits are extensive; nearly fifty of them written in sprightly manner without being cutey-cute.

That news letter was far better than the first one described, yet even it could be improved probably fifty percent simply by having a professional touch — which our hypothetical PR person could quickly inject in a manner which to him or her would be simple routine.

The "Guest Editorial"

One very fine component of church news letters, too infrequently used, is that attention-getting feature called The Guest Editorial.

People all like to have their say, church people especially like to "put in their two cents worth." Very well, let them. Invite your congregation to volunteer guest editorials. You may get none at all at first, and have to coerce somebody into writing one. But when the idea catches on, you may be so flooded with offerings that an entire Guest Issue of the paper will have to be produced.

If you give all editorial writers **carte blanche** you may live to regret it. I recall one crusty old biddy who wrote a "piece" for the paper at my church when I was temporarily the editor. In it she called the pastor a liar, then in another said that the choir director should not be seen "making eyes at" the new college-age contralto. Well, the preacher was not a liar, he just disagreed with the author. And as for the director — I couldn't see why he **shouldn't** make eyes at that lucious looking college girl; I had the same impulse myself, as did every other honest man in church. But the director was unwed and so was she, and what business was it of that old biddy in her pew, anyway. I threw her editorial away, and she acted a little cool toward me for months. In place of that editorial, I printed one by Otto Schmieder titled LET'S MAKE THIS CHURCH GLOW AND GROW AT CHRISTMAS. Otto, reared a watchmaker, was skilled with his hands, and wanted to do a grand job of illuminating our building for the holidays. The Power Of The Press? It still exists! We put on such a light show that December as to warm the hearts of everybody in town. I remember that Phil Hart, a professional electrician, was moved to give four solid days to stringing wires, painting scenes, placing floodlights and spots, making the central patio a soft blue-lighted wonderland.

So — judgment; editorial discrimination. You, the editor, cannot be a mealy-mouthed Casper Milquetoast, nor can you be a Butch Bulldozer. Talk with your people there in the coffee hour. Listen to them — and when you sense a good topic for a guest editorial, wheedle that surprised person into writing it. Give him/her a word limit, always; about 300 words — one typewritten page, double-spaced — is about a maximum. Encourage frankness, but not destructive criticism. You will find that such editorials quadruple the publicity value of your paper because they get it quoted and talked about.

Write Yourself a Grand "Column"

Probably the most readable feature that you could publish in any monthly church newspaper would be the editor's own "Column." There is abundant proof.

In this, you the editor sort of let yourself go, in a half-zany, but cordial and loving and really high-level, pattern of thinking and phrasing. Moreover, it is easier than you think.

Allocate from 10 to 12 column inches for this, at least. Make a special hand-lettered title; something like PATIO PATTER, or maybe TOWER TALK. One I know about is called WHEE, THE PEOPLE! and believe me it is first-turned-to, first-read, every month.

Below the title, appear a succession of very brief, terse paragraphs. Each contains a nub of humor and/or philosophy, related to the church wherever this is feasible, but often just pertinent to family living or life in general. Name names, when that seems feasible; quote your own parishioners, your church staff, even the sexton now and again. Quote the adolescents, the junior set, the Sunday School teachers. Quote Shakespeare, Plato, Martin Luther, the President in Washington, the mayor of your town, anybody else.

For something like twenty-five years, I have prepared full pages of material like that for several big national magazines. One of them is that regular last page in **Better Homes and Gardens** titled "The Man Next Door," although it is under a pen name (office owned) and is now prepared by the church staff. It still uses the fictional characters that I used there for sixteen years. Similarly, I had a page in the old **Presbyterian Life,** now replaced by **a. d.,** titled "Family Man." Again — for about twenty years I wrote "Gong and Gavel" in **The Kiwanis Magazine.** Since about 1956 I have had a monthly full page in the finest church journal of all — **Home Life**. There, it is titled "Let Father Speak." Its popularity is downright phenomenal. Readers by the hundreds write me of their lives, their loves, their vows, their hopes; one Christmas Season brought in more than 8,000 Christmas Cards and I loved every one of them. Many of those missives had poignant heart messages inside. By corresponding with one teen-age girl "fan" for a year or so, I saved her from suicide. For many another person, I am often a sort of father-confessor, a valued friend even though contacted only by mail.

All of that tells **you** something, Mr. Church PR Person. Which is why I have detailed it here.

It tells you to go thou and do likewise, on the local scene.

It is a thoroughly **tested** editorial technique, in building reader interest and response and come-back-again-next-month. I guarantee it — such a department will quickly become the primary feature of your monthly church letter if you write it not off the top of your mind but from the bottom of your heart.

The content for such a "column"?

Within reason, the sky is the limit; just so long as it has a definite format of the proverb or the epigram. No genius is required; just a sense of humor, a love of people, and a sensitivity for what is wrong and what is upbeat and right in our world.

To encourage you, and show you more specifically what I mean, I reproduce here a selection of typical paragraphs from my own columns:

"You shall love your neighbor as yourself." For all Christians, that's a marching order.

***

"What counts in life," says our beloved pastor, "is what we learn right after we think we know it all."

***

There is no time like the pleasant.

***

"No no, Junior," my friend Bob Orben told his little son, "the streets of heaven are not necessarily paved with gold. Oil, maybe."

***

We know when the Pilgrim Fathers landed. But in these difficult times, we often wonder why.

***

Whoever first said this was a genius:
There is no greater fallacy than to think you will surely do at some future time the better things you are capable of doing now but neglect to do. **Good intentions long deferred lose their vitality.**

***

Overheard at the church social: "Nobody can say anything bad about Helen Hale." To which Mrs. Effluvia Sumppump replied, "I agree. Let's talk about somebody else."

***

"The best thing a father can do for his children," our pastor, Dr. James John Prototype, told us at Kiwanis Club, "is to love their mother."

***

You want classic authority for enthusiasm in church work? Okay, Cicero told us that "In nothing do men more nearly approach the gods than in doing good to their fellow men."

***

"Attitudes," says beloved Ralph Yates our head usher, "are more important than facts."

***

You have nerve trouble, emotional disturbances? The three greatest tranquillizers are good morals, good exercise, and good humor.

***

"Those who will not remember the past," said George Santayana, "are condemned to repeat it."

***

The trouble with trouble is that it often seems like fun at the outset.

***

A real Christian is a man who never gets caught cringing at the bottom of the boat.

***

It is imperative that we Americans now develop a Philosophy of Quality. Too long we have worshiped quantity.

***

They smiled when you arrived on earth. Don't let them cheer when you leave it.

***

Nothing is discussed more and practiced less than prayer.

***

You think you have troubles? Last night my water bed caught fire!

***

Religion is like a bicycle; when it stops going, it falls over.

***

"Christianity is like football," says our local high school coach. "You have to grab it, hold it tight, run hard with it. Or something will tackle you and throw you for a loss."

***

When all else is lost, the future remains.

***

I could fill this book and another like it with such readable little quips and comments from my pages in magazines. Maybe I should! I have had literally hundreds of requests for such a book. No no, friends, I did **not** originate them all; in many instances I am what is called a "benevolent plagiarist," meaning that many are "swapped" or picked up here and there from other people. Wherever I do know the originator, I give due credit, but too often I can't learn his name. But there is a sort of unwritten law among us epigrammatists and yarn spinners, a friendly agreement that we may use each other's stuff without credit, within limits; especially where our audiences do not overlap.

Once I published that magnificent quatrain about living —

Live-and-let-live was the call of the old;
The call of the world when the heart was cold.
But live-and-HELP-live is the call of the new!
The call of the world with a dream shining through.

Isn't that lovely? Wonderful to read, to recite, to hear, to meditate upon, to quote from? Also, to reprint — with due credit — in your own monthly church news letter, Mr. P R man? Go right ahead and repeat it. JUST BE SURE that your printer does not omit the name of the poet, Edwin Markham, as my printer did!

For your purposes, Mr. PR man, the long and short of it is that any Church News Letter must be something looked forward to. That's when it becomes a powerful force in publicity for the church.

But it must be envisioned and created by persons with imaginative flair. It must have an innovative editor, preferably one who is slightly audacious, and never, never "afraid." Yes, a few people's feelings may occasionally be hurt by something he prints. If not, he probably isn't printing much of anything worth reading.

Chapter 7

THE SERMON OF THE MONTH

Hundreds of churches across our English-speaking world, and even in foreign-language nations, make a practice of printing the minister's sermon of last Sunday, then stacking copies at the doors for people to pick up as they leave the sanctuaries this Sunday. Very often a little bowl is there, with a sign that says ten cents, twenty-five cents or similar.

Investigation shows that fewer than thirty percent of the worshipers, on the average, do pick up copies of those sermons, although most of those will dutifully drop a coin.

A poll of the people who have picked them up reveals that "No, as a matter of fact I seldom do read them, at least not all the way through, or maybe I just skim them. But I somehow feel that I ought to support the idea, even if I don't get around to giving them a thorough reading and study."

So there you are. Good Dr. Prototype's last-Sunday discourse is dutifully printed and offered, but very little comes of it.

I have already explained why very little comes of it; the spoken sermon loses its salt when it appears in print. It is almost totally without the pastor's personality projection, which is so vital to anyone who would preach. The written word is always different from the spoken word, if it is to be effective. Preachers, orators in general, tend to "get bogged down in the effervescence of their own verbosity," as the saying goes. Our ears tolerate that; our eyes do not.

Do Not Print Every Sermon

Much experience by churches across America and Canada has proved that printing **every** Sunday's sermon is sheer waste. Doing so not only is costly but the sermon quickly becomes too commonplace, the pamphlets command minimum interest and use.

A far better policy is to advertise a carefully selected **one** sermon out of each four or five.

Tell the people, verbally and in print, that Dr. Prototype's magnificent message on WHAT THE RESURRECTION MEANS IN OUR TOWN AND TIME has been unanimously chosen as **The Sermon Of The Month**, and will be available in printed form — so long as the supply lasts — as you go out the doorways next Sunday.

Appoint yourself a few benevolent "shills," Mr. PR man. You and they "talk it up" during the social hour, at church dinners and such. Plant in everybody's mind that they can indeed have a free copy of that sermon of the **month!** As long as the supply lasts! Its very designation implies exceptional worth. Suggest that it be read and discussed in group meetings everywhere — folks at church gatherings are forever needing "devotionals," you know. See to it that copies of the sermon are posted on bulletin boards, placed in hotels, libraries, and schools, free. Build its importance, give it a strong pitchman's come-on.

Prior to all that, when you start preparing the copy for your printer, be absolutely sure that you have a tightly edited, condensed version of his sermon. This for instant and maximum impact on the readers' minds.

To that end, give Dr. Prototype's first typed version the same hardboiled condensation treatment that **The Reader's Digest** gives to the manuscripts they buy. That magazine will pay a fat fee for an article that runs 5,000 or more words, either an original or a reprint. But in The Digest it will have only 2,500 words or less, yet somehow the "meat" of the piece has been retained.

The short length of your printed sermon is quickly read, easily assimilated. Where space permits, the Bible text for that Sunday may well be added, as a separate unit from the sermon proper. So do get right down to the nuts-and-bolts of his discourse when you print it. Use short sentences, short paragraphs. Also it is best NOT to suggest that people pay for these printed Sermons Of The Month. True, they must be done on high quality paper, with maximum eye appeal, high dignity facade, preferably in larger type than usual for easy reading. But what would you gain by collecting a few coins in that little bowl at the door? Let the church budget you generously for public relations work. The pleased people will always more than make up the cost when they sign their next pledges. Generally, low church pledging has always been due to low-level church performance anyway; enthusiasm opens pocketbooks.

Spread The Word

The Sermon of The Month from almost any church can be filed permanently in libraries and homes, so plant that idea among your people. It should by all means be filed in the church library itself. What, your church hasn't one? Well, sir, move into that at once! Every modern church needs an active church library, with constant public-relations publicity to encourage its use.

Send copies of the Sermon to the local newspaper editorial writer (not the news editors), also to the radio and TV commentators in your area. You will be surprised at how often Dr. Prototype will get quoted.

In short, make it high quality, and it will make a welcome for itself everywhere.

Chapter 8

SIGNS, MAIL SERVICE,
PAMPHLETS, CHURCH DIRECTORY

There are endless other types of little public "notices" and leaflets and advertisements and announcements and general attention-getters that emanate from church offices around the world.

One recent December, for example, a stranger offered me a really pretty hand-lettered sign on cardboard about 10 by 15 inches. Red, green, and gilt words on it said

HAPPY BIRTHDAY
JESUS!

Somehow that sign intrigued me. I let him tape it to the inside of the rear glass on my automobile, right-hand corner. The thought of displaying such a sign may be as old as the calendar for all I know. But never before had I seen any kind of card saying, "Happy Birthday, Jesus." This one seemed so very nice; so appropriate and right!

I hadn't driven three blocks with it before a motorcycle officer pulled me over, put down a leg and looked in my window, helmet and badge gleaming. Oh-oh. I must have violated a law.

He shot me a sunrise smile and said, "Them there is my sentiments too, mister. Merry Christmas!" Then with a flourish he roared away.

Within the two miles to my home at least four or five people in their own cars saw my sign, pulled up alongside and waved or gave me approval motions with their fingers. One bearded teen-ager shouted "Right on!" All the ensuing three weeks were like that; dozens and dozens of people expressed their approval. A filling station man called all his help out to read that sign, then said to one of his fellows, "Go right now and paint **us** a big sign just like that, then hang it out front where that Texaco sign is now. Hurry!"

Happy Birthday, Jesus! Well why not! That's what the celebration is all about, isn't it? So why hasn't Hallmark or some other big firm offered us millions of such sign-cards for mailing and posting in our everlasting gratitude for the birth of God's own Son?

Meanwhile, why don't **you** Mr. church PR man, somehow produce a multitude of such signs and cards for distribution every December hereafter? No, do not, ever, let them appear "commercial." Do not allow any to have "Courtesy of Umpth National Bank" on them or any other credit line — except.

Down in one corner of the sign, barely visible from two feet away, print this:

The Downtown Church of The Chimes
urges you to join us in celebrating.

Use small type. Just enough to let people know that your church (by whatever name, of course) is sharing the grandeur of Christmas.

Beware Of Other Signs

That is the **only** "church sign" of which I approve at the moment. I don't even care much for those stark bulletin boards stuck on posts on church lawns, though I suppose they serve a purpose. I don't think it helps much to post cheap, moveable letters out there each week, giving the pastor's name and degrees, stating the next sermon topic, adding maybe a silly wisecrack as some churches feel impelled to do. ANY signboard in front of a beautiful, landscaped cathedral, or even in front of a tiny Little Brown Church in The Wildwood, is an eyesore abomination. Some words chiseled in stone, maybe, or done in wrought iron or brass, should give the name of the church in subdued manner. One such adds GOD WELCOMES EVERYONE, and I can't argue with that. But billboards as a category of advertising are in such ill repute everywhere, that the church should assuredly help campaign against them. I envy Honolulu; you never see a blatant sign of any kind in that great American metropolis; the women of the town long ago just clamped down on the city fathers who would have allowed signs, and they still maintain a sharp lookout.

Similarly, bumper stickers have had their day.

JESUS SAVES was a popular sticker for a few years. But affixed to any car, right away it became mud splattered, scratched, faded, desecrated in general. That's true of all other bumper stickers. And once on, they are **there**; the ony way you can really get rid of any horrid looking bumper sticker is to sell your car and buy a clean new one. The church cannot afford cheapness. I have a hunch that God dislikes billboards and bumper stickers that detract from the beauty of his world.

The Degradation Of Our U.S. Postal Service

It is shameful.

Indeed it is embarrassing.

I am writing this in the latter part of the 1970s, and week by week, month by month, the once magnificent United States Postal Service keeps sinking lower and lower. Among the organizations hardest hit by that have been the churches and synagogues of the land.

We Protestants are going to have our annual congregational picnic on the shore of beautiful Lake Whatchamaycallit? (That's an old Algonquin Indian word meaning "I forget your face but I remember your name.") Then let's mail a postcard announcing it to every family. Thus we all lived in faith; childish faith that our semi-sacred Postal Service would never let us down.

I have some penny postcards. They date from 1921, collector's items. Their counterparts — as of this writing — cost **nine** pennies. By the time you read this the cost may be up. And they are still poor little 3-1/2-by-5-1/2 yellowish things at best, as "cheap" looking as they were in 1921. No progress has been made.

Even so, we are a habit-ridden population, therefore hundreds of church offices still mail "penny" postcards for special announcements. And the sad part is not the specious cheapness of cost, it is the minimal impact that such cards have on recipients. They now have an appeal roughly comparable to that of advertisements addressed to "Occupant." They **are** advertisements, and they **look** like advertisements, hence hundreds of thousands of them are barely glanced at and not read at all. Even when read, they connote little; they carry no subtle aura of quality. And high quality absolutely must become the hallmark of everything any church does, if it is to keep up the prestige that is inherent in its "merchandise." What we the churches are "selling," remember, is the very highest quality of all the products in the world.

Let the PR man therefore come up with a larger card printed as a folder on fine, heavy paper stock. Let it show a classy photograph, preferably in color, of Lake Whatchamaycallit, along with a sketch map of how to get to the picnic grounds. Let the text matter glow with dignified, informal enthusiasm.

No, Mary Lu cannot create such a mail piece, any more than she could write that news copy for the daily **Clarion**. She is not trained for it, and is too busy anyway. But the PR person is trained for it, has the necessary instinct or "feeling" for this and all other public appeals. So by all means let him/her do the job, and not pinch pennies while about it. This admonition applies whether it is a picnic or a prayer meeting, a ladies aid conference or a baseball game.

Do Not Flood The Mails

One point should be remembered — too much of anything, tends to kill its value. Many churches, overly-enthusiastic but under-qualified, mail out something every week, even in this era of outrageous postal charges. But we must realize that a fifty-year **plague** of unsolicited mail has caused almost all of it to lose impact on its recipients. Time was when a direct-mail advertiser could expect ten percent or more of his mailing-list people to order something by mail. This has dropped under five percent and is still going down, because our mail boxes at home are jammed with junk each day.

Any church piece, therefore, must be a standout. Tests show that one piece a month is about a maximum allowable for any church, if we measure costs against results. Many churches have substituted telephone campaigns for costly floods of mail.

For Hotels, Motels, and Camps

One excellent publicity outreach used by many churches with conspicuous success is beamed at travelers, tourists, vacationers, and new residents.

Almost every community, however small, has an inn. This of course dates back B.C. There was one inn where a young couple asked for a room and none was available, and the poor innkeeper said that the only spot he had for them was a stall in the barn, but it had clean hay in it and — well, you know. In modern times our mother country, England, developed highly picturesque inns with picturesque names and traditions, but in our own land — posh hotels, motels and even boatels, plus endless mobile-home camps.

We need to contact all those good people with our church outreach. Very often, the Gideons have placed a Bible in their rooms, and the results from that have been fabulous. But such travelers also need a local contact, a direct, warm invitation to attend church service, to meet friendly folk in worship and social fellowship.

Wherefore many churches today, especially in resort areas, print or lithograph special invitations to such travelers. These are usually in the form of slick paper folders, made to fit the standard racks found in the offices of such places. Surely you have seen the rows of maps, hotel advertisements and similar in those racks. Very well, then, envision an **especially** attractive one placed there inviting people to church.

Use that fine color photo of your church building as a start for designing the folder. Careful wording also is essential. Start it with this important approach:

We urge you to attent the church of your choice. Our area has many fine houses of worship, for all faiths. But if you have no other preference, we cordially invite you to our rather wonderful

DOWNTOWN CHURCH OF THE CHIMES
400 block on Maple Avenue
(See map below)

That church-of-your-choice phrase is vital. It tells the stranger, and the other denominations in your town, that you are not being invidious or narrow-minded.

Make the remainder of the text matter brief, informal, and informative. Do mention the Social Hour after morning worship — travelers often get homesick-lonely. Do mention Sunday School, and nurseries for any babies, and parking spaces. Do mention that your pastor(s) will be glad to counsel strangers on any special problems. In short, make it clear that your church is active and friendly all the way.

A routine for distribution must be set up, refilling the racks as needed. Teen-agers can help with this. Place folders in all hotels, all motel and camp offices, also at the front reception counter in the Chamber of Commerce, in the public library and its branches, in all the banks that will allow it (and most will, because they maintain a welcome service of their own) and in real estate rental offices.

Supply copies to that happy Welcome Wagon lady. She calls on new residents in town with advertisements and small gifts from merchants. She is always a diplomat, and can do wonders for you. She may not charge the church at all; so, Mr. PR man, be sure to take her to lunch, buy her a pretty corsage, and invite her to your church. Come to think on it, Mr. PR man, you have an exceedingly pleasant job, all the way; you are doing good, you are "white collar," you are largely your own boss, and you meet The Best People. What more could you want, man! Or if you are a lady PR expert, those assets still hold. Count your blessings, both of you.

Your Church Directory

One last church publication will be considered here, but it is highly important, and all that has hitherto been said about quality still applies.

It is an excellent idea to publish a **Church Directory**, then update it at least once a year.

This lists, alphabetically, each family in the membership. It includes street addresses, zip codes, telephone numbers. Every member of every family should be listed, including the newborn babies.

It does not take an expert to do this. Most of the details are already on file in the church office, but an updating by telephone usually is required. Sweet Hermina, the elderly volunteer, and two or three of her friends, would enjoy making such a list for the printer. (Don't forget to take those ladies to lunch too, Mr. PR man; you be a gentleman — hear?) Do stress that detailed accuracy is imperative. A name must not be listed merely as Hube and Bonny Jones. Make it Hubert W. and Bonita Marie (Hube and Bonny) Jones. Or maybe she spells her nickname Bonnie, so find out. Details! Carefully thought out, carefully typed, checked and double-checked, both on the original typewritten manuscript, then repeatedly on the printer's proofs before going to press. Absolute accuracy is a must.

Make your directory in the form of a pretty booklet, maybe 4 by 6 inches, surely no larger than 5-1/2 by 8-1/2; it's an advantage to have it fit easily in a lady's purse, experience reveals; certainly nothing like the large-format telephone directory.

Photographs of the people?

Forget them! In the first place, it is impossible to get every member's photo; some folk just will not cooperate. If you set up a portrait studio in the church itself, a minority won't come there even if it's all free. And of those who do turn in pictures, at least half are dissatisfied with the way they look. Which is only human nature; I myself am far, far more handsome than my best portraits reveal — I swear it! If you hire experts to retouch out my old-age wrinkles and my turn-downed mouth, the cost skyrockets. Finally, a number of us will die before the Directory is revised next year, and that requires a costly revision of many pages. So just forget about a photo directory, even if (as often happens) some smooth-talking itinerant photographer wants to take every member's picture free and give you a copy. What he **really** wants, of course, is to sell expensive sets of prints to his victims. Eschew him. (I could have said avoid, or shun; but this here is a very scholarly compendium, and we scholars never use a short word when a bizarre long one will do).

It is traditional to publish the pastor's photo on the Directory cover, or surely on Page 1 just inside. But there is nothing sacred about tradition, certainly not here in the last quarter of the 20th century. That preacher is well paid — or should be. He doesn't need, or even want, a lot of hoked-up prominence; that's old-hat stuff. People come to church to worship God, not Dr. Prototype. This kind of talk maybe shocks you? All right, friend, but I am being realistic. One thing that our churches probably need above all else is operational common sense, divorced from foolish precedents.

Art Work, Then?

I love good art. You bet I do. But there is art and art. In your reach for excellence, Mr. church PR man, don't "art up" your Directory (or any other church publication) with too much phony abstract or even impressionistic stuff. Modern church architects, notably, have almost gone berserk in designing our tabernacles, and so have many national headquarters offices in designing leaflets and propaganda tracts. Symbolism is fine, but be wary of cultural snobbery when using it. Which reminds me — yes — of a story!

There was this little sweetie-pie girl, about eight years old, hence very sharp minded. She somehow got into a big museum of modern art. She paused before a large framed painting that showed nothing but outrageous splashes of black and green with bits of blue, all whorled and entwined beyond human understanding — you know the type of thing. I suspect it was even beyond divine understanding. And she just stood there spraddle-legged, fists on hips, gazing up at that mess.

The curator saw her. So he walked over, smiled fatuously and said, "Darling, that is supposed to be a pretty pony galloping across the prairie."

Whereupon little sweetie-pie glared up at him and gave the ultimate art criticism. She said, "**Well, why ain't it, then?**"

Make the cover of your Church Directory attractive. A good start, as with that folder for the motels, might well be to use those color plates reproducing the photograph of the church itself. The words "DIRECTORY OF MEMBERS, Downtown Church Of The Chimes" might be imprinted on that. One way or another, make it eye-appealing as well as practical.

Just inside, do list the names of all pastors, assistants, secretaries, Sunday School officials, any other staff persons, with addresses and telephones. That becomes a simple convenience.

State the current dates and hours for all meetings. List any special groups such as Boy Scouts, Girl Scouts, Youth Groups, Clubs for Middle-Agers and Old-Agers, whatever your church offers. Print those, along with the membership names that follow, in fairly large type for easy reading; don't try to skimp just because this is the church. Church skimping is a fallacy, always, no matter what the endeavor or the project is.

Finally, beloved Public Relations man or woman, keep one fact firmly in mind: **a lot of people will disagree with you and your thinking, your plans to upgrade every aspect of your church.** These will voice criticism; they will talk behind your back.

Their type also voiced criticism of Jesus and talked behind his back, but he just went on about his Father's business, doing what his mortal intelligence told him was best for all concerned.

Chaper 9

TELEPHONE, TELEVISION, RADIO

One of the greatest advances man has made since he chiseled out the first wheel came when a 19th century American stuck his head under a blanket on the floor of a room and said aloud — "Mr. Watson, I want you."

It might have been Jesus calling. One way or another he calls each of us Mr. Watsons every day.

It wasn't. This was a slightly "teched" screwball-genius mortal. He spoke into a little gadget about the size of a tin can. A wire from that gadget extended from under his blanket, through a wall, and to a similar gadget held by a man under another blanket on the floor of the next room. And lo — the real Mr. Watson in that second room, **heard that call over that wire!**

Impossible! Unbelievable! Maybe even sinful; if God had wanted man to talk over wires, he would have given us — what? The zealots of that day were confounded, as well as dumfounded.

All right. Today we hold a somewhat nicer little gadget in our hands (my wife's is called a Princess Model), touch a few buttons on it, and talk with perfect clarity to almost anybody anywhere in the world. A god's blessing, beyond words. I still don't quite believe it, certainly don't "understand" it, because electricity and electronics in general baffle me even though they do not baffle my ten-year-old grandson.

Happily, I do not need to understand — nor do the public relations experts in our churches. We — they — just need to **use** the telephone for the advancement of Christianity. There are countless effective ways for them to use the little gadget now.

In passing, it is interesting to note that even the phone we use today is obsolete. The phone of 1999, I am told on good authority, very probably will be about the size of a pack of cigarettes and will be strapped to your wrist. Press a few tiny buttons. A signal leaps from you to Telstar to Telstar to a similar telephone on the wrist of your friend in Kamchatka or Kalamazoo, Johnsonville, Texas, or Johannesberg. You will see each other's faces on your wrist phone, in full color and 3-D. You will then talk with each other as casually as you now talk with your family at the dinner table in your home.

Impossible? It is already definitely tested and in production plans.

An even more discombobulating truth is — even **that** telephone may not materialize because — hold on tight, now — marked advances are being made in **Thought Transference!** That scares me a little. Imagine, being able just to "tune in" on your wife or your husband by somehow adjusting your brain, and communicate across the continents and the seas. I refuse to discuss this. I mentioned it to that hepcat ten-year-old grandson, and that rascal merely shrugged and said, "Sure, why not?"

For Now, Struggle Along With What You Have

Okay okay, Mr. PR man, for now let's just use the poor little old horse-and-buggy telephone device that we do have. But keep one fact in mind — its use for the church must be done with careful discrimination.

All across our nations today, folk in their homes are harassed by pests who telephone while we are at dinner table or — with uncanny accuracy — at other inconvenient moments, to offer us a carpet cleaning service, sell us a bargain photo if we will just come in tomorrow, teach us dancing lessons for only $5 down, on and on. We soon come to abhor these annoying callers and all they represent. Thus the church callers dare not slip into their despised category.

When calls for the church do seem advisable, let the PR person give out a list of callers with many personal friends in the congregation, with requests to call those friends alone. "Hello, Margaret? . . . . This is Hazel Bancroft, and I have a very special message for you from our church . . . . Yes, we **are** all fine, thank you, and how are all **your** family? . . . . That's wonderful, Marge. I'm so happy for you. Say, we must get our families together. How about hamburgers on our patio this Saturday night? You ask Tom; no, you **tell** him, and the children of course. Informal. Just dips and burgers and pop and stuff. Badminton afterward. Fine, fine! Saturday about six. But right now, Marge honey, I have been asked to remind you that our church Women's Association will meet for cake, coffee and conversation on Friday at 10 a.m., and we want you to give us a short devotional. You are so good at that, we just love the way you can think on your feet. I will ask Lillian Gaines to pick you up — okay?" . . . . You know how it goes; The Girls, on the telephone; the church Girls, ages 15 to 95. Conscript them, bless their feminine hearts.

There are two sides to that calling coin. While many of us get too many nuisance calls, we all welcome honestly friendly ones from our church or about its activities. Moreover, a great many members get too few calls of any kind. You would be astounded to know what lonely, isolated lives many nice folk do live. They just are not outgoing enough to command much attention, they are the Forgotten Ones of human society. These — bless them — even enjoy the salesman-pest calls, because it breaks the monotony of their days.

Such types also make expert callers. Because they are eager to serve the church — did you realize that? In addition to enjoying the human contacts that accrue.

So — a frequent discriminating use of the telephone can work wonders in public relations for any church. Such calls show that the church **cares**, that the member is treasured. Thousands, millions, are led into joining churches — then are promptly just dropped, neglected, forgotten with no follow-up, and lost again. That is stupid church programming! Let that marvelous desk gadget serve your flock, Mr. PR man. In effect, put your head under a blanket and in Jesus' name say to the people — "Mr. and Mrs. Watson, we want you and yours. Because you are cherished, you are loved."

Dial 494-Pray

Positively, that is a valid, active telephone number. If you live near Laguna Beach, California, dial it and see. Or from any distance, anywhere in continental America, put the 714 area code before it then dial; the small toll charge will be worth the moment of goodness that you hear. Night calls, midnight to 8 a.m. especially, will be very cheap indeed.

You will hear a short, beautiful, helpful, recorded prayer. From that Riviera Town Of The Pacific, specifically from a downtown church that does indeed have beautiful chimes ringing out every quarter-hour every day, to the infinite pleasure of the people.

In that church, the service is called PRIVATE PRAYER. Hundreds of thousands of people have used it, because so many of us feel the **need** of prayers, yet are unsure of ourselves in attempting it on our own. Millions are like that, you know. And even those of us who do approach God directly with our hearts and words, can listen profitably when an eloquent clergyman speaks for us.

In my other church, the larger one at Phoenix, the same service was installed about twenty years ago, with one telephone hidden in a far upstairs third floor attic closet, dark and locked. No human attendant was, or is, necessary; the mysterious thing is completely automated. Each morning, as in Laguna Beach, a new prayer is recorded for its callers by one of the clergymen on the church staff.

In Phoenix the service is called DIAL-A-PRAYER. Same things as Private Prayer. It is in use around the world.

I remember once when I was alone in Wiesbaden, Germany, feeling lonely and homesick and baffled and worried about a family matter, unable to think clearly. I sat in my hotel room, brooding. By chance I glanced at the telephone directory on the table there. In both German and English language on its cover were the words DIAL-A-PRAYER and a number.

On impulse I did dial the number. I heard a **click**, then a melodious if slightly gutteral voice began **"Unser Vater in dem Himmel —"** and continued the prayer that Jesus taught us, then added some comforting words of the speaker's own. I spoke a little German, I mean I understood enough to catch the majesty of that opening Lord's Prayer, and most of what followed. **Click** again, followed by silence.

That short prayer in the German language, that one "impersonal" contact, refocused my mind away from self, out of deep introspection and self pity and worry and fear. I am never by nature an anxious or cringing person, but I suppose troubles can break down any of us. Anyhow, at that very moment I slowly stood up, recited The Lord's Prayer in English, opened the hotel window, stared out at the marvelous landscape, undressed, went to bed, slept soundly all night, awoke at dawn refreshed in body and spirit. And lo — before noon the family matter had been completely resolved.

Yes, I could have prayed solely on my own. No, I do not, ever, cotton much to ritualistic printed prayers or rote-like verbalizings from somebody else. I **do** pray on my own; often several times a day, with the preponderance of my praying, silent or aloud, given to thanksgiving. Yet I fully recognize the value of what is called intercessory prayer, too, that being what Dial-A-Prayer really is. Psychologically, it is help beyond measuring, as millions of telephone users have come to recognize.

I cannot learn who first dreamed up the idea of recording prayers for the telephone, but all honor to him or her. "Is it popular?" you ask. Well, ten days after we first installed that one telephone in Phoenix, we had to add another because so many hundreds of "busy" signals showed on the automated report. After thirty days, four phones were in that closet, operating side by side, just to handle the thousands of calls for prayer that came in each twenty-four hours. And the service had been given relatively little publicity in print; news of it had just spread happily by word of mouth.

Such a service for your church must of course be arranged with your local telephone company, but that usually presents no problem. So by all means offer it in your area. Not even a paid public relations person is necessary to start that; Mary Lu or Dr. Prototype or the sexton or any delegated person could see to it. The community will bless your church when you do. It is one of the nicest, sweetest bits of outreach ever conceived.

"Good Morning Mr. and Mrs. America, Let's Go To Press!"

Remember? . . . You older readers? . . . Back yonder not too many years ago? A fast-talking Jewish gentleman named — let me think, what was it? He was a famous newspaper columnist who also came on the air with machine-gun words of gossip about politicians and movie stars and their ilk, wore a snap-brimmed hat all the time, a nice guy — WALTER WINCHELL, that's who!

Oh . . . Well, Walter was the epitome of broadcasting back yonder when **radio** was in its heyday. You know — radio; which was positively killed forever when television came along — remember? Good old Walt would come on each evening and grip everybody from the Gaspe Peninsula to Baja, California in the Pacific sea. I mean, radio was that good. It was marvelous. You Johnny-come-late children and grandchildren don't know what you missed.

Well, I have good news and bad news for you. The good news is — radio did **not** die when TV came along. It slumped, then bounced back stronger than ever because — now for the bad news — television slumped even worse, due to the complete frothiness of its many programs plus the utter silliness of its far-too-many commercials.

For our purposes here, the big point is that radio offers limitless possibilities in publicizing the churches and upgrading our nation spiritually. Which is the whole ambition behind this book.

We church folk have too seldom grasped radio Opportunity by its forelock. But there have been many wonderful exceptions. Let me now detail a very special, fascinating experience in this field.

In airing a combination of preaching and choir music, nothing has ever been more imaginative, more dramatic, more popular, than that famous Easter dawn radio broadcast from the south rim of the Grand Canyon. For many years the National Broadcasting Company carried it to affiliated stations around the world, even to ships on distant seas. It was inter-denominational, ecumenical, Christian. It came as a half hour right out of the thin nerve-tingling air of northern Arizona. The altitude there is about 8,000 feet, so that the people who go there are so close to the famous Rim that they are in some danger of falling a death-dealing mile down to the Colorado River.

One year the radio people talked my close friend, Ronald Bridges, Ph. D., into delivering the Easter dawn sermon up there. Ron was not an ordained minister, but he could out-preach half the men who were. He was a high-level college professor out of New England, brother of the famous Senator

Styles Bridges. Ron had come to Arizona seeking relief from arthritis (but did not find it, poor soul). He was so brilliant, so humble and devout as a lay leader, that his Congregational Church made him its national boss, called Moderator. So, when NBC tagged Ron, that Easter program was already an assured success.

Okay. He slaved for weeks on the manuscript for his sermon. He bulldozed me, an author, into helping him with phraseology and stuff. Together we tightened it, marked in spots for emphasis, timed the total to the split-second as required by radio.

"I will be very mike-frightened," said he, then. "So will you please come to the Rim with me and stand at my side before the microphone when I read this sermon?"

Certainly I would. A friend is a friend, and I loved this one even if he **wasn't** a Presbyterian — as I often teased him. If I could be any help on that Rim I would be right there.

We spent that Saturday night in a deep-freeze vault widely known as El Tovar Hotel, right on the very edge of the cliffs. Broadcast was set for 6 a.m., when the Easter sun would throw its first golden spears over the thirteen-mile wide greatest natural wonder in the world. At 5:30 a.m. we walked out of the hotel and started shivering in a frigid, penetrating wind. Broadcast point was a quarter-mile away. When we got there, we were frozen zombies. So, too, were all the choir members and radio technicians numb with cold.

Nevertheless "the show must go on." With a high wind snatching at everybody's clothing and hair, freezing our skins and our enthusiasm, the choir sang **a capella** as best it could. That same man whom I have mentioned earlier, Howard Pyle, the radio man who became Governor of Arizona, stepped to the microphone just six feet from the sheer rock-rim drop-off. With a few trembly words he signed on Dr. Ronald Bridges.

Stiff with cold, Ronald and I had been crouching close together behind a nearby pinon bush. On signal he stood up, I with him as requested. We took the five steps to the microphone. He removed his typed-and-timed sermon manuscript from his pocket and was about to begin reading.

At that instant, the hard cold wind snatched the manuscript from his hands and scattered it like confetti over the Grand Canyon of the Colorado, a massive gorge unmatched on earth.

Ronald turned to me, his "helpful" friend. His mouth hung open in horror, his chin bobbed as he tried to say something but couldn't. The typed sermon was irrevocably lost, while hundreds of millions of people around the world awaited its opening words. Mike fright? I would bet that no other human being ever experienced it more acutely.

There was no choice. So with gestures to his lips and quick finger waggings, I ordered him to **speak!** Just start, man; say anything!

Whereupon Ronald Bridges, Ph. D., the distinguished and nationally renowned Congregational layman, merely delivered the grandest Easter sermon the world's radio listeners have ever heard. He spoke **ad lib**; from deep in his soul.

The world at large never knew of his problem there, of our intense shivering cold, our loss of the manuscript. The sermon that he did deliver seemed twice as good as the one that we had laboriously written. Letters by the thousands came in testifying to the grandeur of that dawn discourse.

Publicity value? Who could possibly measure it? I would just have to repeat that nothing has ever exceeded or even equalled it since Marconi first sent a few faint dot-dash sounds a short distance through the air.

"The Song of The Meadowlark and The Babbling of Brooks"

You good folk who read this will not likely have opportunity to brave a microphone and talk around the world. Yet what you **can** do locally is priceless, too. We have four or five times as many radio stations today as we had when Ronald spoke, television notwithstanding. As with TV, radio has a voracious appetite; it gobbles up all the "good" programs it can find or contrive — hence welcomes any happy surprise that offers itself.

Offer it some surprises, Mr. church PR man.

Just remember that this is a new, modern day. The best-selling Bible of the century is one titled **Good News For MODERN Man**. But "modern" is not really the key word in that title; the word GOOD is. Hence your cue is — so to speak — not to emphasize the crucifixion in your church radio broadcasts, but the Resurrection!

Many traditionalists cling to the notion that a worship service must be not only decorous and dignified, but gloomy and sad as well. That premise is and always was absurd, and definitely it did **not** come from The Bible —

The hope of the righteous shall be gladness.

Whoso trusteth in the Lord, happy is he.

Thou hast put gladness in my heart.

Thou has made known to me the ways of life; thou shalt make me full of joy with thy countenance.

Behold, I bring you good tidings of great joy, which shall be to all people.

I challenge you — show me any sepulchral tone in those famous quotations! Jesus set in motion a faith that was happy and joyous and exciting; a laughing, lilting religion, if you will. In early centuries, the wise people already realized that; they described Christianity as "the song of the skylark and the babbling of brooks."

I cannot, here, detail any specific program for use in individual towns and cities via radio. I don't need to; you the PR people can dream up better ones, because you are on the local scene, you know and love your neighbors there. Mine likely would be Pacific-Ocean oriented, but yours might be a fine Wisconsin town, or a Gone-With-The-Wind setting in Atlanta, Georgia. Make your program relevant to the people in your own area. Just be sure that it is optimistic and upbeat and good-news in tone. If what you broadcast is not good news, it is not Christianity.

Some church radio programs have been about 99 percent sacred music, and this has much to recommend it. Just look how that famous Mormon Tabernacle Choir comes across the air, nationally! Hundreds of trained voices, broadcasting out of Salt Lake City, singing from their hearts. The publicity value of that is greater than money could ever buy. In fact I would say that of all the Christian sects in America, the Church of Jesus Christ of Latter Day Saints (Mormon) is the most enthusiastic and most successful at advertising or public relations.

It is never easy, however, for the church PR person to round up, rehearse, and present a group of talented choristers on radio. If they must be paid, costs run too high. If they must be volunteers, conveniences and obligations elsewhere must be considered. Hence an **occasional** musical show on the air is about all most churches can hope for; maybe once a quarter, or at Christmas, Easter, and sometime in early autumn.

One simpler type radio program that can be offered in standard thirteen-week or even daily programmings, is called the Devotional. Many churches already offer these. Such a program is not an evangelistic whoop-and-holler thing, not an emotionally hopped up performance at all. It is rarely even a categorized sermon. Rather is it more nearly comparable to the grace prayer before meals. It is short; fifteen minutes of it is enough. A clergyman with a good voice and stage manner comes on the air and just "talks." No blatant exhortations or hellfire-and-damnation warnings, and yet no nanby-pamby soft soap, either; Christianity is, truly, a religion for strong people; for weak people whom it makes strong. Each talk may be followed by a quick invitation to visit your Downtown Church Of The Chimes or whatever, then join its membership if the listener feels so moved. Do not let your speaker labor that invitation; look to the broader good, the over-all grandeur.

Very often such a series of talks — whether on radio or television — can be taped in advance, corrected or improved where need be, aired once, then syndicated to other stations in non-competing towns. The taped radio talks also can be used by your own and other churches on play-back machines for shut-ins, in hospitals and in homes.

Do Not Strain To Use Television

There's no doubt about it — television is an electronic miracle. It came so **suddenly!** Man trod the earth for thousands, millions of years, discovering fire, inventing the wheel, domesticating the camel and the horse, the chicken and the dog, chipping out stone points for his arrows and spears, developing the crossbow which a Pope declared would soon destroy all mankind because it was so deadly, catching electricity on a kite string, hoisting cloth to move boats, on and on. Yes, man advanced swiftly from the time he crawled out of the primordial slime, changed fins to feet, got the divine spark from God and started really **living**. From that date to A.D. 1940 was a stretch of — five, ten, fifty million years? Paleontologists can't seem to agree on the time since Adam and Eve appeared, but it was a long, lon-n-n-n-ng stretch. That Grand Canyon alone took nine million years in the digging, they tell us. I had a close friend named John C. Lincoln, a preacher's son of the Victorian Era. As a young man he worked a while for an electric shop in the midwest, but one day the boss fired him, saying, "John, get out of here and better yourself. Electricity has gone as far as it ever will or can go, there is no future in it." Circa 1890. John went on to found and develop the great Lincoln Electric Company in Cleveland, with branches around the world, biggest electric-welding enterprise ever known. But even he didn't live to see television.

That miracle was non-existent on Monday; on Friday — so to speak — it sat in every home across the American and Canadian nations. And you dare tell me there have been no miracles since Christ ascended into heaven?

You well know how wonderful this one is. What most church workers do **not** know is that television is not really their metier.

It takes an incredible mess of preparation to put any television "show" on the air. All kinds of technical fummadiddling has to go on behind the scenes, and in the studio itself there is nerve-straining make-ready. Experience proves that not one "church program" in twenty is really worth airing on television. They lack those essential intangibles that make the TV program a success. Such as surprise element, alert timing, personality projection, general verve and excitement. An effective TV program must **grab** the viewer-listener and **hold** him, it can never be a relaxed, lackadaisical sleepytime half hour, surely can never tolerate a sepulchral **doloroso** atmosphere which too many preachers and other church folk feel is necessary and appropriate.

Wherefore, Mr. PR man, you are advised not to strain at "getting your church on television." You simply haven't the talent nor the time nor the money nor the need. Maybe, later, say about 1990, it will be feasible for each major church to have its own television broadcasting station — there is much talk of such already. So do keep an open mind, and if opportunity pops up suddenly, lasso it! Television appeared overnight, church use of it may appear in the next five minutes, relatively speaking.

There are some exceptions. In a few cities and towns, churches have already used television to advantage. But in such instances, special conditions exist. Just investigate your local situation carefully before you plunge.

One very probable development, real soon, is that many, many churches will be able to fire their second and third-rate preachers and buy first-class preaching piped to their sanctuaries from New York City, Chicago, Hollywood or somewhere. Down front in the sanctuary, at the chancel, will be a large screen. At the right moment, the current Billy Graham or Norman Peale or Bob Schuller or other really brilliant pulpiteer will appear standing behind **his** pulpit, and he will give us a sermon each Sunday that is truly inspired. Maybe it will be a woman preacher. Frequently it will be His Holiness The Pope himself. There is no limit to the Great Ones we could pipe into our sanctuaries, by cable for absolute perfection of image on the screen. In which case the average preacher, who is far more eager than able today, will be relegated to **ministry** rather than oratory; he can call on the sick and lonely, he can become a clinical psychololgist to help his troubled flock, he can work with and for the young people in Sunday School, he can keep busy for 26 hours out of every 24 if it gets to time-on-duty. But we won't have to sit in our pews, bored and tolerant, listening to him preach.

I look forward to that day.

And don't try to tell me it won't work!

Of course, it will work! If a shallow-brained comedian can stand on my home screen for twenty minutes and hold my rapt attention, a deep-brained clergyman could certainly hold it in my church sanctuary. Definitely, without argument, the human personality can and daily **does** come through perfectly via television. Graham, Peale, Schuller **et al** are proof that preaching comes through as powerfully as comedy does.

Chapter 10

STUNTS, DISPLAYS, SPECIAL ACTIVITIES

You may not believe it just from my telling.

But come next August into northern Arizona, climb the high rock mesa to the oldest continuously inhabited town in the U.S.A., the picture book pueblo named Oraibi. Find a soft comfortable rock in the town center, then just sit there and wait. Pretty soon

— — —

From an underground meeting room called a **kiva** will stream a big group of Hopi Indian gentlemen. These citizens of America, quite dark of skin, muscular, with face chiselings to delight any artist or sculptor, will wear no conventional clothing. Mostly they will be attired in breechclout, armlets, anklets, moccasins, and paint, with a few feathers here and there.

As they step from the **kiva** ladder, they will string out single file and start a rythmic dancing — **while holding long live venomous rattlesnakes in their hands and mouths!**

The sheer hideousness of that spectacle will shock you, yet you will stare at it, spellbound. The Hopis have been doing that each August (the exact date varies, so check on it in advance) for many centuries. And no, the deadly reptiles have **not** been de-fanged or milked of their poison. And yes, the dancers positively do get bitten, on hands, arms, chests, even faces. Don't ask me why they suffer no ill effects; even the most avid scientific researchers have been unable to answer that. Snakes re-captured by paleface herpetologists after being turned loose by the redskins, always have fangs, and poison sacs are intact except for those few that have just bitten an Indian. There are fascinating details about that renowned Hopi Snake Dance if you are further interested.

For our present purpose — just know that it probably is the most bizarre and revolting **religious** stunt known to mankind today.

Yes, religious. Almost everything the Hopi Indians do is associated with their religion (in which trait we might well emulate them). In this incredible instance, the dancing ends and the men race downhill onto the near-barren plain, scatter in all directions, and release the snakes unharmed. Those hideous things are construed to be Little Brothers Of The Rain Gods, and the ceremonial dancing is really a prayer for life-giving rain. Released, the snakes carry the plea to the unseen gods.

Well, well, and who are we palefaces to criticize? We in **our** zeal have placed beautiful living maidens on stones and disemboweled them, and — do I remember that God himself had to stop a certain fellow from destroying his own son? We have thrown living persons into fiery furnaces and off high cliffs. We have fed them to vicious hungry lions while we sat sipping wine and laughed at the spectacle. And yes, we in our modern time, today, have in the name of religion cavorted with live, venomous reptiles in our hands, but **we** are not immune, and the poison has killed some of us; just two days before I wrote this, a court judge has had to make a stern ruling about our use of reptiles, because two dancers died from their fangs. Paleface dancers, mind you, in the good old intelligent U.S.A.

Advertising (or publicity) has been defined, correctly, as "proclamation, for getting attention."

Do you follow me, ladies and gentlemen?

Don't Try It!

No, I am not suggesting, Mr. church PR man, that you stage a rattlesnake dance for the public in the patio of your Downtown Church Of The Chimes. It might get considerable attention, at that! But there are bright people and stupid people on earth, just as there are good people and bad people, and generally there is a marked separation in each case. It falls to the bright ones and the good ones to do the separating.

Not by any stretch of the imagination do we intelligent church folk dare permit any kind of stunt or display that is repulsive or dangerous or ugly or has any other manifestation of the crackpot, immature mind. People have slept on sharp upended nails in the name of religion. I know one modern "Christian" sect whose members, during Lent, strip naked and flail themselves mercilessly with whips and thorny cactus limbs as they creep toward the local church. Those too are members of an Indian tribe, primarily; some are of mixed blood.

But, lest you misjudge **all** Indians from this sketchy adverse report, I hasten to add that most of our aboriginal citizens belong in that classification I called bright people, and good people.

Consider, for happier instance, the Navajos.

Now **there's** a tribe! To my thinking, it is the most intelligent of all. They faced the same outrageous treatment that we whites gave all redskins during the 18th and 19th centuries, but they wouldn't be licked, even though no less a personage than Kit Carson tried it. Under a famous leader, our bureaucratic military rounded up all of the then existing Navajos, about 8,000 of them, and hazed them like cattle on a deliberate 200-mile "death march" then turned them loose on a cold and barren reservation, confidently hoping and expecting that all of them would soon die there. The only good Indian was a dead Indian. This, mind you, was done with federal government and general social approval, by people considered to be civilized white Christians.

Those few near-freezing, near-starving Navajos refused to die. By 1970 their numbers had increased to 120,000 proud Americans. They also had become the richest redskin ethnic group on the continent. When palefaces were sending money to support puny little Christian mission churches on other reservations, they finally started one for those modern Navajos. Whereupon the proud Navajos themselves donated $25,000 toward constructing a really fine new church! At that moment their tribe, controlled by a strong Council, had a reserve rainy-day fund of $2,000,000, and no indebtedness. Which was exactly $2,000,000 more than the esteemed paleface United States Government had, not to mention its astronomical national debt.

Mrs. Navajo is a great weaver of rugs (often miscalled blankets.)

When she weaves, sitting cross-legged outdoors before her log-and-mud hogan (pronounced HO-gahn) home, it is a poetic spectacle for all to enjoy. She chants a little, low tone, as her shuttle is zipped with the woof through the threads of the warf. She is using wool that she and her daughters have grown on family sheep, have clipped, washed, dyed, spun, and blessed with loving hands. Adele and I, in our big Indian pueblo home that we built of adobe bricks in Phoenix, had about 30 Navajo rugs, one of them measuring 11 by 14 feet. Each of those rugs took months in the weaving, the large one about two years. Now, get this: the Navajo squaw weaver has absolutely no pattern to work by except in her mind. The resultant design is always very intricate, with many diamonds, angles, rectangles, cornstalks, figures of sacred dances, whatever she can contrive. As she weaves, she rolls the finished part on a small log, and never unrolls it for study again; yet the finished portion is in absolutely precise duplicaiton of the starting point, right down to the last thread and bit of color! For all those months, she must carry that detailed mathematical count, that color pattern, for repeating later, in her mind alone. It is a phenomenal performance, from an "uneducated heathen Indian woman."

The big pay-off is — every detail in every rug, is of deep religious significance to its weaver. Those designs and figures are symbols of her contact with the Divine God of us all. She is not "stunting," not showing off, not being commercial, not working for money in any sense even though she may later sell her rug. She is, instead, worshiping. **And is advertising her beliefs!**

Are you worshiping when you sew up a dress, madam?

Are you worshiping when you sell insurance or groceries or automobiles, mister?

The Navajos are worshiping with virtually every move they make. Religion dominates in the weaving of rugs, or in the men's production of America's Only Crown Jewels, the exquisite turquoise-and-silver bracelets, belt conchos, necklaces, earbobs, rings. When you build a home, Mr. and Mrs. White American, do you **always** place its only door toward the east in order to welcome the Sun God? Do you face Bethlehem whenever you kneel to pray, as the Moslem faces Mecca?

Meditate on all these wonderful concepts, Mr. church PR man, when you consider the excellent potential of "stunting" as a means of church publicity. In Arizona, white churches often bring in a fine Navajo woman and let her do her weaving on the church lawn or patio, for all to enjoy. She frequently is a Christian herself, in which case she may weave in some of our beloved Christian symbols; but this is rather rare, and such rugs jump sky-high in price because they are collectors' items.

Two wealthy eager-beaver members of the Masonic Order came to Arizona as tourists and saw a talented squaw weaving. They were fascinated. Through a white trader, they arranged for her to weave them a very special huge rug to be placed on the wall of their big Masonic Lodge back east. They paid in advance, and said they would pick up their rug a year hence.

"We ask just one thing," they told her through the interpreter. "Please weave our Masonic Square and Compass design in the center of the rug. It is quite sacred to us."

She agreed. She went to work, then she started thinking — I am doing this rug for paleface men. They have asked me to weave in something important in their religion. But it is only one thing. So what else can I find that is sacred to the palefaces and would please them if I wove it in?

So okay, folks. When those two dudes from Detroit or somewhere picked up their Navajo rug next year, they had a priceless one indeed. Mrs. Navajo had cast about looking at the landscape along the transcontinental highway nearby, and found something else "sacred" to the poleface brain. Beside that meaningful Square and Compass, she had woven in a big red blatant Texaco Gasoline sign!

Immortal Advertisers at Work

I could cite you a thousand other strange customs, episodes, incidents, and stunts from around the world, showing what mankind has done and still does to "advertise" or publicize beliefs that are close to the heart.

Why was Joan of Arc willing to let herself be burned to death publicly, if not from some profound inner conviction which she hoped others would acquire?

Why was John Calvin such a rebel, unless it was for reformation of a religion he felt was supreme?

And how about that strong-willed young monk named Martin Luther? He was born November 10, 1483, and "little reckt he that he would change the world." He and his parents alike probably figured that he would just grow up as another routine peasant. But one day when he was a youngster, a bolt of lightning struck the earth near him, scaring the unholy bejabbers out of poor Marty. "Have mercy, Saint Anne!" he yelped in terror, and I don't blame him. "Protect me, protect me!"

All right, she did; or God did; without knowing it he was destined for Big Things. As his mind matured he began doing some deep thinking, and this soon caused him to buck the Establishment, the hierarchical powers; he spoke in protest against certain practices and beliefs. When the high-ups ignored or scorned and threatened him, the now 34-year-old Martin got mad.

So he wrote himself 95 academic theses on "The Power Of Indulgences" and boldly nailed them to the front door of the Schlosskirche (castle church) in the town of Wittenburg, Germany. Maybe he didn't really expect much to come of that youthful expression of rebelliousness; likely somebody would just tear those theses down and that would be that.

But you well know what did result from that publicity stunt! He posted his these on October 31, 1517, and on October 31, Protestants around the world will still be celebrating those protestations. Publicity, advertising, holy ballyhoo, is just that strong in potential; you never know when some bit of it will revolutionize a life or a nation or a world.

Dream Up Some Modern Ideas

As with staging a snake dance or weaving a sacred rug or burning someone at the stake, or even nailing a bunch of theses to a door, modern stunting is a combination of mysticism, fanaticism, and heaven knows what other isms. The human mind, which is the ultimate computer, is stranger than any electronic gadget we will ever know. Theses? Written in figurative blood by one man? Heavens, today we Efficiency Expert Americans would appoint a committee to do it! It would in turn appoint six sub-committees and they would all fummadiddle around for nineteen months, and hire nine Philadelphia Lawyers, ask for and get large government appropriations, endlessly read the minutes of their last meetings, get rather high salaries all the while (with retirement pensions and other fringe benefits, of course) and eventually come up not with a mere 95 succinctly written theses, but with 1900 pages of un-understandable ecclesiastical gobbledygook.

Martin said precisely what he knew to be the truth, in as few words as possible; much as God did when he gave Moses those Ten great "theses." And as with Moses' Ten — just look at the results!

Brevity of Action, then, not prolonged pageantry or pontifical proclamation, should be your guideline for The Downtown Church Of The Chimes, you publicity people. Let me now Cite Another Instance.

One recent autumn, the publicity man in my own church developed a moochy stunt. ("Moochy" is a Mexican border colloquialism, based on **mucho hombre**, or much man, hence tags anything admirable or good.) When we worshipers entered our high-vaulted sanctuary that Sabbath morn, lon-n-n-n-ng silken strings extended straight up from the end of every third pew. Atop each string was a large helium-filled balloon — iridiscent reds, pinks, greens, yellows, blues, glistening in beauty against the delicately tinted ceiling. We worshipers must have showed our surprise, but we just bided our time.

At the end of the morning service, the pastor told us that each balloon had a tiny message printed on it — "Praise God. Please write (church name and address). We looked up at them with renewed interest.

"Now," said the pastor, "will the person nearest each string please detach it, roll the balloon down, and carefully carry it out into the north patio. When you get there, tie it to a child's hand. Several lovely refreshment tables have been set up under the trees, with cake, coffee, and punch. Each table is presided over by one of our newly-elected deacons. Carry your balloon to that table with any child you find. Greet the new deacon and enjoy fellowship for a few moments."

We obeyed him, and it was a happy time. Soon the patio was glowing with bobbing balls of beauty; alive with chatter and laughter and fun. One sweet old gal did venture a criticism; she said she felt that such a display had no place in the holy sanctuary or patio. But nobody paid much attention to her; we were all admiring and marveling. Many cameras began to click.

Next, the pastor came to the top of the steps at the sanctuary door, lifted his arms, smiled big, and started singing "I am the church, you are the church, we are the church together." We joined him with zest. At the end of it, he yelped — "NOW, children! Let your balloons go free!"

It was exhilarating to see hundreds of balloons shoot upward, pass the treetops and the red-tiled roof of the church, catch the ocean breeze and head toward the nation's Original Thirteen States. Suddenly everyone was cheering, laughing, pointing, chattering, and altogether enjoying the spectacle. It was much like the releasing of balloons by college kids at a football game, it created a contagious excitement. The pleasure continued for more than half an hour longer, with fellowship the highest ever.

Whereupon that fine old lady critic smiled and told her friends, "Well, I apologize. You can't argue with success!"

She was right; you can't. Success is its own vindication of effort, any time. Maybe even for those outrageous snake dancers — they are successful in keeping **their** religion alive. Besides which, surprisingly enough, after those dances it nearly always does rain!

We were so taken with that balloon show that we immediately demanded that it be repeated on Easter Morning. Except that, on Easter, the printed message would be "CHRIST IS RISEN!"

Many of those first balloons were heard from in due time. Half way across the continent in Arkansas, a farmer wrote, "A pink balloon settled in my pasture and a message on it said 'Praise God.' I hereby do just that, and I thank you Californians for sending me your blessing."

How wonderful are thy people, O Lord. And our colorful, refined, inexpensive, picturesque, spectacular "stunts" that help spread news of thy loving kindness and forgiveness of sins. May we never "judge" other groups of worshipers whose methods of advertising their religions are not precisely like ours.

Try That Balloon Show

By all means use that balloon display if you wish to, gentle readers. Then originate other stunts of your own. Collect yourself a committee of Source Minds. Maybe the first stunt suggested will evoke a negative reaction, and some jerk will grimace and say "I wouldn't touch it with a ten-foot pole." Very well, then, develop an eleven-foot pole. Never let one thrower of cold water extinguish your fire.

Brainstorming sessions, notably with high school and college age youth in them, usually generate more good ideas than you can use. What one member says somehow stimulates thinking in another. Before you realize it the abstruse knowledge has been tightened down into something for delightful, concrete action. That kind of mass thinking has not only virtually eliminated small pox and diphtheria, it has even sent some of our men to that well known desert, the moon.

Let's hark back again to Easter and think a little. What can we do there? Easter, you know, is not **just** a day to wear flashy new clothes, doze through a routine sermon, sing the Hallelujah Chorus, and traipse on home. It is the peak moment of the Christian year; yes, I think it exceeds even Christmas, because it was the triumphal climax for the Babe.

Could we begin our observance on Good Friday? How about having five or six fellows costumed as Jesus' and working in shifts. Let one don his robe, put on a crown of thorns, lift a cross, and appear to be straining under it there on the church lawn on Good Friday. Just frozen there, motionless, a living statue.

When that was done, you should have seen the reaction! People at first seemed appalled — and well they might. Then they became silent. They paused to stare, doubtless also to think, meditating on the message. The crowds grew. The word was passed around and still more came, a steady stream all day. A silent sermon for the multitudes. A glimpse of the Via Dolorosa, 2,000 years ago.

But on Easter morning, that cross was erect — and empty!

What can you and your committee dream up about the use of rabbit eggs, Mr. PR man?

Rabbits — bless the little hippety-hopping endearing creatures — are too smart to lay ordinary white or maybe speckled eggs, they are shrewd enough to lay eggs in colors that match those balloons. Well surely, that is a tee-off point for something beyond the conventional hide-and-hunt in the shrubbery. Work with the Sunday School teachers. What can be done with and for the school's pixie set? I don't want to tell you, here. **You** tell **me**! I'm working alone, I don't have a brainstorming committee, but you do.

Or consider Christmas once more. Surely, surely, everything that was ever possible in the way of celebrating Christmas, has already been done — hasn't it?

Of course not. Christmas with its pageantry is the very best opportunity you will ever have to advertise your church and its message. Tradition makes it dominate Easter, rightfully or not. Of course we think instantly of decorations. Then likely we move on to re-enactments again, from outdoor Nativity scenes to in-the-sanctuary pageants.

As I write this, one church is planning to erect a special sign for next Christmas Season. It will say that grand greeting —

"HAPPY BIRTHDAY, JESUS!"

by using thousands of those tiny "firefly" electric lights which in recent years have been used extensively in outdoor trees. It will slowly flash on and off. Every five minutes, a recording of young voices will sing out to the passersby —

"Happy Birthday to you,
Happy Birthday to you,
Happy BIRTHday dear Jesus,
Happy Birthday to YOU!"

Can't you just imagine how the hurried-harried Christmas shoppers will pause a moment for that, smile, and feel exalted? Public relations!

The Calling Pastor

Almost every church has one. Usually, a senior gent, kindly, benevolent, understanding; one who feels for persons who are sick in homes or hospitals, some permanently bedridden. May God bless that church worker! He is vital to the life of any church in his direct person-to-person outreach. He is always welcome; indeed his call is looked forward to, eagerly.

Let yours never become a Sad-Sack type, sanctimonious, preachy, pietistic, dull. Most aren't, but some are. May he also use the radio? You bet he may! Almost any station will provide him free Reach-Out time, especially at Christmas Season. Thus he can spread his happy influence far beyond his own parish. See to it, Mr. Public Relations Man of Woman; help him schedule that air time.

Other Tested Stunts

Since about 1960, our grand old church in Phoenix has maintained a continual art show in its large, beautiful main parlor. People stream through there after each worship service on Sunday.

So called "religious" art is not favored, although there may be some religious subjects at times. High class canvases are preferred, but an occasional "Sunday painter" is allowed to "hang" in there. The city's best artists have been there, and felt honored. Many sales have resulted. The church charges no commission, but the artists often become generous on their own. Money is not the real consideration. The real one is that good art is beauty, beauty is close akin to love, love is close akin to Christianity, thus good art can publicize Christianity, and many good artists do not have adequate exposure in the first place. A service, in all ways.

Other churches that I know of have frequent art shows like that and also have occasional craft shows. People from their own memberships, plus people from the town population in general, bring in their finest work in macrame, brass, iron, wood, stitchery or whatever, exhibit and sell it and see it admired. The church is encouraging happy artistic outlets. The church is saying that we are glad to make this a center for successful living among friends who are understanding and kind.

I doubt if you could dream up a better public relations thought, Mr. expert PR man.

In certain rural or village churches, such things as chicken shows, turkey shows, dog shows, cake-bake competitions, sewing exhibitions, even horse shows, log splitting contests and church-painting picnics, all are fairly routine. They invariably add up to fellowship and fun; they say, again, that the church is the center of my life.

In the somewhat broader field of church activities, picnics, hikes, horseback rides, motorcades, boat tours, mountain climbs, swimming parties and such, are not only very common, they are priceless in public relations. The Puritans, the Pilgrim Fathers, went to church to pray and maybe sing a little but mostly to hear sermons that often ran three hours long. The late-20th-century Christians go to church to pray, to sing for joy, to hear a sermon for guidance, and to join in fellowship activities that enrich the quality of their living routines. Thus your measuring stick, Mr. Behind-the-Scenes public relations man.

Off my hometown coast of Southern California we have — of all things — a happy annual Whale Watch. You heard me — Whale Watch! It is infeasible for you good folk in Arkansas or Manitoba to stage a church whale watch; you just don't have too many whales there. But we have scads of them. Each spring they stream down from Alaskan waters by the thousands, moving to a specific bay near Baja, California to give birth to their calves. Papa whales tag along, I suppose just for the sport of it, maybe because they love their mamas, as we of **homo sapiens** do. So we go out in boats and watch.

There they come, slowly slipping along, arching up to "blow" then inhale, submerging with a high graceful flip of their beautiful tails, swimming under water for a bit then repeating the age-old, endless water routine. Just resting, they look like huge submarines. Because they are so enormous — would you believe fifty tons — they are not dangerous; they mind their own business and we mind ours. Sometimes we speculate on which one it was that Jonah swallowed; I mean to say, we have a great deal of fun and frivolity and fellowship, whale watching. We take the church kids along, and the grandparents. We snap photos, and share them at church supper next week.

Friends in San Diego a few years ago caught a baby whale and made a special city pond for her. She became a sort of state pet. We named her Gigi. When she grew too big for domesticity, we laboriously trucked her to a boat thence out to the sea and dumped her into the stream of those big swimmers. At first, she felt lost, confused. Then Gigi joined them, and each season now the little radio device which we affixed to her hide broadcasts news of her reappearance nearby. Maybe Gigi has had a calf or two by now. The kids in our Sunday School all drew stylized crayon portraits of Gigi and her hypothetical babies.

"The Ten Most Wanted Men"

You know about those. The FBI issues their names and photos, and most ultimately get caught.

Well now, consider Bob Harrington, an evangelist in New Orleans. In 1969 **he** published a list of **The Ten Men Most Wanted** — for leadership in winning followers for Christ. How about that!

He spoke right out plainly, as evangelists are wont to do. I mean, Bob named names. That year, he said the Ten Most Wanted Men in America for Christian leadership were Howard Hughes, Jimmy Hoffa, Don Drysdale (ex-baseball pitcher) Frank Sinatra, Dean Martin, and some lesser Names of the moment.

In 1976 his list was headed by Muhammid Ali (who calls himself a Muslim), Hugh Hefner (who developed the Playboy Clubs and Playboy Magazine), Johnny Carson, Elvis Presley, A. J. Hoyt, Evel Knevel, Joe Namath, Howard Cosell, Walter Cronkite, and Henry Ford II. Evangelist Harrington made the definite point that he was not "judging" those men, but that "I'm just saying that if they spoke out for Christ they would have great influence on the nation."

The idea is fascinating, you'll have to admit!

True, I hope **my** pastor never issues such a local list; he'd probably start it alphabetically, and I'd be right on top!

Even so, any church Public Relations Expert can "play around" with that idea. He could use it, or have it used, as a veiled threat in his own town or parish — even though no names actually were ever published. The point being — it would cause talk; interesting, vivacious, recurrent talk among The People. Which, after all, is what a Public Relations Expert always wants most. Word-of-mouth.

The Church Building Itself

Before we move on, hearken to this fact: the structure itself is an advertisement — what else? Why do you think those devout people in Salisbury, London, Cologne, Paris, Rome, Chartres, all around the world, have spent billions of dollars and many centuries, constructing cathedrals so huge and ornate that they literally awe us, overpowering our emotions even when we just walk by them? For "publicity," of course.

For centuries the Catholics were in the forefront of that. Which may have been due to the fact that the Catholics were, still are, expert at collecting tithes and other monies from their members. Also they were in no hurry; some of those great cathedrals took two centuries to build, and a few aren't even finished yet. We protestants are impatient. We want to lay a foundation in January and have the great tabernacle ready for use by next June. But we are learning. For instance, that incomparable "Vatican of the Protestants" which pastor Bob Schuller is building for half a billion dollars in congested California has been allocated not three months but three years for completion. It will probably take six!

Whatever **your** congregation does, let it be sure to make the church attractive, appealing. It need no longer be "traditional;" in fact it had better not be. The conventional pointed spire with cross on top was great for grandpappy and grandmom, and better yet if under it was a colonnade with arches curving toward the front door. But as we have so often heard lately, heaven does not necessarily have a front door with a Gothic arch.

Most Catholic congregations today are leaning away from the overly ornate cathedrals, those with endless exterior gargoyles and curlicues, endless interior frescoes and saints. One main reason is cost. The people of the 12th to 19th centuries had time; time to work endlessly, for a pittance. Today, we have no time; we must get things done at once, or so it seems. That problem also faces the Protestants.

But good publicity effect can be and is being brought about by modern, unique styling in church architecture for all faiths. Yes, some of it seems kooky; much too bizarre and overdrawn. That's because the controlling boards of the churches and synagogues do not ride strict herd on the designers; church architects, given full freedom, tend to go far overboard, experimental. The Lutherans, notably, have suffered from that. Simplicity is still a cue, as in all art. This applies to exterior landscaping, which is vital also. Any place of worship must be **beautiful** per se, also in its setting. Flowers, shrubs, trees, vines must be planted and tended with perpetual care. Because the millions of people passing by get an impression of grandeur, or of lethargy. Let your Public Relations Expert be hep to all this.

When people speak about that wonder world of beauty called the Deep South, I frequently hear mention of a girl who seems to be named Miss Azalea Trayle. The way I get it, she is very active each March organizing hiking parties and motorcades, not only for tourists but for church congregations as well.

Well, bless her. The South is not fully appreciated by the Nawth; never has been, since Mr. Robut E. Lee tried to explain things to the Yankees. But I have repeatedly gone on flower walks with Miss Azalea and her friends, and believe me there is nothing in America to exceed it. Honolulu and all of Hawaii have grand flowers — that state ought to be up here between Mississippi and Louisiana — but not even my own California can match The South in Spring, hence church flower walking down there is, I mean — prime!

Okay, friends, the serious fact is, almost every town has beautiful flowers in season, and a flower walk from the church on three or four Sundays, with brown-bag lunches toted along, can end up as an unforgettable experience. Florida is a great place for that. So is East Texas. From one of those to the other, in March, the azaleas, dogwoods, redbuds, and endless other glories are on lavish display. Are you listening, Chamber of Commerce people and church people in Savanah?

Service Club Meetings In Church

What would you say is the greatest ethical advance of the century?

In America, the answer is definite — the rise of the service club movement; the growth of Rotary, Kiwanis, Lions, Exchange, Sertoma, Optimists, Ruritan, and many other men's groups that meet once a week for the surface purpose of food, fun, and fellowship, but also for the grander ideal of unselfish service to mankind. Their membership in America alone now totals about 3,000,000 men. From them comes the leadership of the nation; typically, twenty-five members of the U.S. Congress are Kiwanians, as of this writing, besides other club members in there, and the stalwarts in all walks of business and professional life wear little service club pins on their lapels. I know what I am talking about, because I have just published a book titled **The Sacred Ninety Minutes** (Portals Press, University of Alabama, Tuscaloosa). It is the first long-range, definitive study of those clubs, world-wide.

Service clubs' activities are, in point of fact, a direct extension of the grand Christian ideal. Hundreds of thousands of man hours, plus hundreds of millions of dollars, are given each year by service club members just in doing good. They themselves not only are unpaid, but they pay for the privilege of rendering those services. They may not even advertise that they are members of any service club. They seek no publicity, no credit or fame.

But they do eat.

Therein lies a valuable cue for you, Mr. church PR man.

Go after your town's service clubs.

No no, of course not — "the church is not a restaurant." But most assuredly, the women's groups in every church seem eternally straining to raise money for this or that worthy cause. Much experience shows that church women's groups are delighted to be hostesses once a week to the Rotarians or the Kiwanians or the Lions or whatever.

Don't overlook the salient fact that those clubs hold the "big shots" of your community. It does no church any harm to have prominent and important men coming there in mid-week. It encourages them to feel church-related, to come for the Sunday worship as well.

Yes, the stomach is the way to a man's heart. And to excellent church public relations.

Chapter 11

IS THE FUTURE HERE NOW?

"And now in conclusion," as the preacher is wont to say, let us assume that — wherever you live, village, town, city, house, duplex, apartment, mobile home — you arise this morning, stretch, go to the bathroom, walk to your front door, reach outside and pick up a copy of a fine newspaper called **The American Daily**. (Or The Canadian, British, Australian, or South African Daily.) As per happy routine, you carry it into the dining room, sit at table, lift your morning cuppa or your glass of orange juice, unfold the paper and start scanning the headlines.

What you already know, and what any new reader will quickly discover, is that this paper is unlike any other ever published. Your copy is not a local city or town paper, it is a **regional edition of a national daily**. If you live in New England it may have come out of Boston; in New York State, out of that megalopolis called Manhattan; in the midwest, out of St. Louis; in the far northwest, out of Nome; in Hawaii, out of Honolulu; in our Mexican border world, out of El Paso. Maybe there are as many as twenty such regional offices. But all will have sharp guidance and partial content coming from a central headquarters, possibly in Oklahoma City or Chicago. Printing will be in clear offset lithography including perfect reproduction of photographs in color.

In your regional edition, local news will be given front-page priority, shared with important national news, and this pattern will continue inside. But news coverage will be vastly different from that normally seen in big-city dailies. This **American Daily** will have an altogether higher concept of what the people of the republic really want to read.

This one will avoid gross sensationalism. It will ignore the fact that Gloria Brass the sexpot movie star has been re-married for the third time to her ex-husband Richard Blowoff. It will not stress routine political chitchat from far off Canton or Ghana or Tibet, or even Washington, D.C. It will not attack any person, prominent or otherwise, with slyly slanted news coverage of his speech and activities. It will not print any dirty-dig destructive editorials. It will offer no stupidly weird, grotesque, unfunny "comic" strips or pages, but will have an abundance of good and clean and entertaining ones. It will have no political bias, but will be exceedingly active at reporting both the promises **and the performances** of politicians. It will expose graft wherever possible, turn a spotlight on every foolishly bureaucratic expenditure. It will demand punishment of all outlaws high and low, and expulsion of all irresponsible police and judges. It will avoid trivia and stress importance, yet without stuffy holier-than-thou attitude.

The paper will be crowded with advertisements, because the circulation of **The American Daily** will be enormous. National advertisers such as General Motors, General Electric, General Foods (by whatever names) will find its use a rare bargain, because the agate-line rate will be low, low, in comparison to the quantity and quality of readership. Local advertisers, in the regional editions, will pay no more, probably less, than old-style dailies charge them, but will enjoy maybe twice as good results.

Such a paper will not be catering to the riffraff of human society. It will be trying avidly to **help** that riffraff improve its status, but will never attempt to coddle or exploit it. In short, this **American Daily** will set new standards in journalism; will command unprecedented popularity and prestige.

Could Be!

The American Daily, regrettably, is merely a daydream.

It does not exist in reality.

It has been "thought about" countless times; brainstormed, discussed, yearned for, even planned. But it has never gotten off the ground, simply because America has never really put its mind to it.

But we could!

We do positively have the mentality for it.

Moreover, we do positively have the money for it.

My own smallish denomination, the United Presbyterians, who number fewer than 3,000,000 members, had no trouble a few years ago raising $50,000,000 for some special project, I forget what. That itself is an awful lot of money, even during the era of inflation.

What if, say the American Baptists and the Southern Baptists — who really see eye-to-eye and heart-to-heart on most things anyway — should "put their shoulders to the wheel" in financing our hypothetical **American Daily**? My stern old Texas father was one of them. If he believed in something strongly — broth-er, it was as good as done! Such is the hallmark of all good Baptists; where something good is involved, you can't stop them. For our paper, the Baptists alone could come up quickly with $100,000,000.

Not to mention the mighty Methodists, who outnumber many other too-fragmented Protestant denominations. Get **them** revved up and — oh boy! In proportion, the same applies to the powerful Lutherans, Congregationalists, Southern Presbyterians, Christian Scientists, Mormons, on and on.

But hold! We perfect Protestants could and would quickly take a genial new ecumenical look at ourselves and show those beloved neighbors of our

plans for **The American Daily**. I can just see it now —
Father Michael O'Hara and Rabbi Walter Goldberg,
steaming up in sudden enthusiasm. Do I need to tell
you how **their** vast memberships raise millions,
billions, of dollars whenever there is good reason?

No, we should have no trouble financing a
magnificent church-controlled newspaper; all faiths.
Not one that specialized in religious propaganda, but
that specialized in sane-and-sensible news coverage,
editorial comment, essays, feature stories, even
fiction, and advertising, of which God himself would
approve.

A dream, yes, but a valid dream.

Let some Genius now arise and spark the
enterprise.

It could revolutionize the whole world of
journalism, **and of public relations in developing the
godly way of life.**

That would hold true even if the newspaper, as
we know it, suddenly became a museum piece — as
it undoubtedly will. The newspaper of the year 2000
very probably will just roll out of a smallish box thing
inside your home. You will not have to depend on the
neighbor's ten-year-old boy, who now "delivers" by
throwing your paper on the roof, or into the bird bath,
or surely far behind the hedge, with uncanny
accuracy.

That box thing will merely be another modern
mechanical-electronic miracle, giving us up-to-the-
moment news every half hour, at trivial cost; an
effective fight-back at television. So, let us move into
that, when the time is ripe, and produce our **American
Electronic Daily**. Positively, the churches have to
weave with the times. Indeed we must not follow the
pace of progress, we must **set** the pace. This is
required by our intelligent concept of public relations.

If we don't set the pace for mankind with more
zeal than ever before in history, the outlaws and the

con men and shysters and jerks and
immature-minded knotheads in general will quickly
come to dominate. I do not predict that — I am no
fear monger, no pessimist at all — but I do issue it as a
sensible call to arms. "Whoever controls the press,
controls the nation," some wise fellow once said. He
was right; the first major move that Hitler made was
to grab control of the news media. His propaganda
machine was stronger, and even more deadly, than
his military machine. We allies had to contrive and use
a more powerful **proper** propaganda to defeat him.
There is great need for proper propaganda in our
late-20th-century world.